COLLINS GE[M]
CATS
a mine of information

...LINS GEM
...assic
...MS
a mine of information

COLLINS GEM
HORSES & PONIE[S]
a mine of information

COLLINS GEM
INSECTS
a mine of information

COLLINS GEM
KINGS &
QUEENS
a mine of information

COLLINS GEM
MUSHROOMS
& TOADSTOOLS
a mine of information

COLLINS GEM
SNAKES
a mine of information

COLLINS GEM
SPIDERS
a mine of information

COLLINS GEM
STRESS
Survival Guide
a mine of information

COLLINS GEM
TAROT
a mine of information

COLLINS GEM
WINE
Guide
a mine of information

COLLINS GEM
WORLD
atlas
a mine of information

COLLINS GEM
YOGA
a mine of information

COLLINS GEM
ZODIAC
Types
a mine of information

THE
UNEXPLAINED

Karen Hurrell

**Consultant:
Janet Bord**

HarperCollins*Publishers*

Karen Hurrell is a writer and editor. She has long been fascinated by all aspects of unexplained phenomena, in particular ghosts and ghost sightings, and has also written the companion volume to this, *Collins Gem Ghosts*.

Janet Bord has written widely on the subject of the unexplained and has acted as advisor and contributor to numerous books and journals. Alongside this, she runs the Fortean Picture Library, specialising in images of the paranormal.

All pictures courtesy of the Fortean Picture Library except:
Bridgeman Art Library: 32, 91. Frost Historical Newspaper Service: 51, 119. Greg Evans: 42, 43, 49, 106. Mary Evans Picture Library: 15, 18, 19, 28, 47, 48, 57, 59, 93, 94, 101, 102. Pictorial Press: 77, 79, 180, 183, 184. Still Pictures: 90, 166. Topham: 29, 31, 34, 35, 36, 37, 38, 39, 41, 44, 46, 54, 56, 92, 95, 98, 99, 100, 110, 121, 127, 128, 139, 158, 173, 174.

HarperCollins*Publishers*
Westerhill Road, Bishopbriggs,
Glasgow, G64 2QT

www.collins-gem.com

First published 2000

Reprint 10 9 8 7 6 5 4 3 2 1 0

ISBN 0 00 710937-7

Created and produced by Flame Tree Publishing, part of The Foundry Creative Media Co. Ltd
Crabtree Hall, Crabtree Lane, London SW6 6TY

Printed in Italy by Amadeus S.p.A.

Contents

Introduction

Whatever the scientists may say, if we take the supernatural out of life, we leave only the unnatural.

Amelia Barr (1831–1919), Anglo-American novelist

THE CLOSER we look at the world around us, the more curiosities we see that defy rational explanation. For all the scientific scepticism, we still have many truths to learn about ourselves and the world around us. Strange and very real events are often pushed to one side because they can't be explained by common sense or modern science.

This book delves into some of the most enduring enigmas of the known universe, including timeslips, hauntings, rains of creatures, UFOs, little people, unexplained vanishings, natural phenomena, alien abductions, spontaneous human combustion, strange beasts and the powers of the human mind. It will take you on a journey through the unknown. From the mysterious sites left behind by our forebears, to the miracles reported to take place around the world, this book examines the events and stories that have taken us to the very limits of our knowledge. Investigations into many cases result in the discovery of a rational explanation, but there are others that continue to defy our understanding. Perhaps in the future we will turn up reasons for some of these phenomena, but in the meantime, we must consider the possibility that they are real.

In many cases science and investigation have solved the mysteries, but there is no doubt that some of the world's most baffling mysteries will remain just that.

One of the enigmatic monolithic figure sculptures on Easter Island.

How To Use This Book

COLLINS GEM THE UNEXPLAINED will tell you everything about the mysteries and facts of unexplained phenomena. It is divided into 10 main sections, covering the different types of phenomena, citing examples, retelling the tales and giving details of scientific investigations.

Part One looks at the various explanations that have been put forward about the unexplained and includes a history of the phenomena. Part Two investigates some key cases of people who have apparently vanished into thin air, leaving no trace. Part Three looks at some of the most famous marine mysteries, including the Bermuda Triangle. Part Four outlines the mysteries of the deep and the wild: sea monsters and man-beasts. Part Five tackles beings from outer space: alien encounters.

Parts Six, Seven and Eight look at the more esoteric examples of unexplained activity: evidence of curses and jinxes, medical curiosities and religious phenomena such as miracles. Part Nine studies evidence of fairies: sightings and even photographs. Part Ten looks at the mysteries of the ancient and natural world: prehistoric monuments that defy modern understanding, the appearance of strange animals, crop circles and other phenomena.

The Compendium discusses the unexplained on film, examines the most famous examples from the last five decades and suggests films enthusiasts may enjoy. Further Investigations outlines websites and books to help you explore the subject. The index takes you straight to subjects of particular interest.

To find out more about ghosts, poltergeists and other unexplained phenomena, see *Collins Gem Ghosts*.

A

B

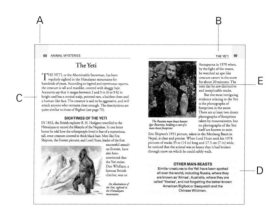

68 ANIMAL MYSTERIES

THE YETI 69

The Yeti

THE YETI, or the Abominable Snowman, has been regularly sighted in the Himalayan mountains for hundreds of years. According to legend and eyewitness reports, the creature is tall and manlike, covered with shaggy hair. Accounts say that it ranges between 2 and 3 m (6 to 9 ft) in height and has a conical top, pointed ears, a hairless chest and a human-like face. The creature is said to be aggressive, and will attack anyone who ventures close enough. The descriptions are quite similar to those of Bigfoot (see page 70).

SIGHTINGS OF THE YETI
IN 1832, the British explorer B. H. Hodgson travelled to the Himalayas to record the lifestyle of the Nepalese. In one letter home he told how the tribespeople lived in fear of a mysterious, tall, erect creature covered in thick black hair. Men like Eric Shipton, the Everest pioneer, and Lord Hunt, leader of the first successful assault on Everest, have also been convinced that the Yeti exists. Don Whillans, a famous British climber, was on

An illustration of the Yeti, sighted in the Himalayan mountains.

The Russian man-beast hunter Igor Bourtsev, holding a cast of a man-beast footprint.

Annapurna in 1970 when, by the light of the moon, he watched an ape-like creature cavort in the snow for about 20 minutes. The next day he saw distinctive and inexplicable tracks.

But the most intriguing evidence relating to the Yeti is the photographs of footprints in the snow. There are at least two dozen photographs of footprints taken by mountaineers, but no photographs of the Yeti itself are known to exist.

Eric Shipton's 1951 picture, taken in the Menlung Basin in Nepal, is clear and precise. When Lord Hunt took his 1978 pictures of tracks 35 m (14 in) long and 17.5 cm (7 in) wide, he noticed that the animal was so heavy that it had broken through snow on which he could safely walk.

OTHER MAN-BEASTS
Similar creatures to the Yeti have been spotted all over the world, including Russia, where they are known as 'Almas', Australia, where they are called 'Yowies', and not forgetting the better-known American Bigfoot or Sasquatch and the Chinese Wildman.

E

C

D

A The page number appears in a colour-coded box, indicating which section you are looking at.
B The aspect of the unexplained you are looking at is indicated at the head of the page.
C The text gives information, examples and evidence of paranormal activity.
D Information boxes at the end of some spreads give further information or examples of the subject.
E Photographs and illustrations show the sites of the activity and the people involved, and evidence of the unexplained.

EXPLAINING THE UNEXPLAINED

Does Science Hold the Key?

OUR COLLECTIVE fascination for mystery is one of the main reasons why our knowledge of the world around us, and the science of man and nature, has been extended. For example, our continued desire to solve the mysteries of space has pushed us towards an exploration of our solar system and beyond. But despite the huge technological advances, much still remains shrouded in mystery. Even today the mysteries of space, coincidence, paranormal phenomena and exceptions to what we consider to be the natural law (the rules of life) remain elusive.

Our fascination for the unknown has led to a desire to solve the mysteries of space.

THE POWER OF THE MIND

DOES THAT make the mysteries impossible? Many scientists would say yes. Others, however, have used these inexplicable phenomena as grounds for increasing our knowledge. For example, we are now learning that the human mind is much more powerful and capable than we could ever have imagined. Telepathy, teleportation, telekinesis, ESP (extrasensory perception) and prophecy are no longer the kingdom of fantasists. We study paranormal activity and ghosts; we have captured mysterious images on film. And although objects have been seen in the skies since ancient times and have been randomly interpreted as divine lessons, signs and tests, UFO sighting is on the increase and has spawned an industry of investigation. The Catholic Church views many miracles as signs from God and we have realised that the rich culture of belief in the unknown that has been part of human life for over 50,000 years has some gems of wisdom within it.

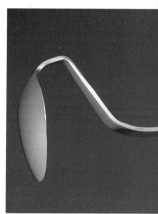

A spoon bent through the power of the mind, known as psychokinesis.

Let's look at some of the theories that have been put forward to account for unexplained occurrences.

Earth Magnetism

FOR CENTURIES, people have sought explanations for the mysterious phenomena that will be discussed in this book. What might cause the appearance of poltergeists, the disappearance of human beings and objects, strange lights in the sky or visions on a hillside?

Just after the Second World War, Guy Underwood undertook a series of experiments. He began to explore prehistoric sites with a dowsing rod and soon discovered that every site has one or more centre or 'blind spring' from which streams run. In these areas an electrical current seems to be present, often taking the form of a huge spiral. Stonehenge, for example, has masses of these currents in spirals and loops. Underwood believed that these electrical forces caused the earth to hold the memory of an event, particularly if it was intense or highly emotional, allowing this event or emotion to remain in the atmosphere. This remains conjecture, but if true, the theory would explain many phenomena, such as the creepy feeling experienced upon entering a graveyard, a sacred place or a haunted house. It could also explain many hauntings and a wide range of natural phenomena such as crop circles.

Dowsing has revealed information about the earth's electrical forces.

Illustration by Leonard Sarluis showing the fourth dimension, in which all things are part of a single whole (1923).

Vortexes

THE NUMBER of extraordinary disappearances on stretches of sea, such as the Bermuda Triangle (see p. 48) and the Devil's Sea, prompted Ivan T. Sanderson, an avid collector of information on strange occurrences, to attempt to find a rational solution. He marked the Bermuda Triangle and the Devil's Sea on a map and observed that the two areas lie in roughly the same latitude and are approximately the same size. Other observations of similarly troublesome areas of sea led Sanderson to conclude that there are twelve zones lying on this latitude around the world. He suggested that the Bermuda Triangle is the most notorious because it is one of the busiest sea areas of the world. He noted that these areas lie in parts of the ocean where warm and cold currents collide, causing 'nodal points' where surface and subsurface currents turn in different directions. He believed this creates a magnetic vortex which draws ships under.

Sanderson went on to conclude that some of these areas must exist on land. Taking his theory further, it may be possible that there are spots on the

Ivan T. Sanderson, who attempted to find a rational solution to mysteries such as the Bermuda Triangle.

The cover of Sanderson's book, Invisible Residents, *in which he explored unexplained phenomena.*

a disquisition upon certain matters maritime and the possibility of intelligent life under the waters of this earth by IVAN T. SANDERSON

INVISIBLE RESIDENTS

earth's surface where such fields are created by freak conditions, manifesting themselves as a kind of whirlpool in our space-time continuum. If so, objects passing too close could be absorbed and then spat out later, although they may be drawn in and never return in our normal space-time.

Sanderson's theory has been widely discounted, partly because it does not offer an explanation as to why some ships are simply abandoned. Perhaps, though, if crewmen were aware of a spiralling force beneath them, they might be tempted to abandon ship, then be sucked into the vortex. The ship could, theoretically, be spat back out, or only slightly submerged. The answer is that we simply don't know, but Sanderson's theory is worth considering.

Blessed Earth?

SOME SCIENTISTS have explored the idea that the earth is alive, with the same type of life force or animating energy that humans have. If it sounds bizarre, consider the fact that acupuncture is now widely accepted in the Western world, despite the fact that we cannot scientifically prove the existence of meridians, or channels of energy that run throughout the body. Does the earth have similar lines of energy? This theory would explain why parts of the earth seem to be blessed while others are cursed. The earth is now considered to be a connected system of characteristics and features. This theory is known as the Gaia Principle and it states that the many characteristics of the earth, such as its magnetic fields, the biospheres of living creatures and plants, the atmosphere etc. are all interconnected. If this is the case, is it not possible that the living earth has the power to create what we consider to be unexplained phenomena? Could this be the first step toward a scientific explanation?

The ancient art of acupuncture is now widely accepted as an alternative therapy in the Western world.

Does this theory also explain strange disappearances and supernatural appearances? Are there parts of the earth that are cursed, coughing up bad luck, if you like? Is this why we experience an uneasy feeling in a particular place, and why we are able to see unhappy spirits or experience highly charged occasions, such as battlefield re-enactments or violent deaths?

If we could understand the laws that govern the interaction between the life's vital force and our own subconscious minds, we could perhaps go some way to understanding the many unexplained phenomena that continue to puzzle modern man.

A man is immersed in the 'miraculous' holy waters at Lourdes.

A History of the Unexplained

ONE OF THE most profound differences between our modern-day culture and those of our forebears and more primitive cultures is the fact that we seek an explanation for everything. Technology and science have given us the where-withal to assume that every mystery can be solved, and that there must be answers to every question. In the past, belief rather than technological know-how led to an acceptance that there are mysteries and parts of life that cannot be explained. For shamans, for example, out-of-body experiences, the power of the mind to heal and to communicate, and the possibility of life after death are all realities. They don't aim to dismiss them, or to explain them. They do so not because they have studied these things, but because they are a part of life. They know

which aspects of these mysteries they regard as having objective, non-personal reality and which are aspects of the spirit and mythology.

A computer simulation showing a Near-Death Experience: a tunnel of light is a frequently recurring characteristic of the phenomenon.

Dr Raymond Moody, a leading authority on Near-Death Experience.

DR RAYMOND MOODY

A renowned scholar, Dr Raymond Moody is the leading authority on the Near-Death Experience. His landmark book, *Life After Life*, was published in 1975 and has sold some 14 million copies worldwide. Moody noted that people who had returned from the brink of death claimed that they had seen a bright light. He collected a group of accounts and showed that this phenomenon was happening more and more in a world of medical miracles, where revival is much more prevalent than it used to be. He defined a common pattern for the cases, some of which exhibited many of the features he had described. Had he proved, with the approval of much of the mainstream scientific community, that there is life after death?

ANCIENT MYSTERIES

THE NUMBER of 'mysteries' appears to be on the increase. We spot UFOs, cases of spontaneous human combustion are becoming more prevalent, we see (and more importantly, perhaps, believe in) ghosts, and we pour millions of pounds into investigating age-old mysteries, including pyramids, miracles, Stonehenge, lake monsters, fairies and vanished people and vessels. Have the number of mysteries really increased, or have we just developed a fascination with the unexplained? Cases of unexplained phenomena have occurred across history, from the beginning of humankind. Cavemen scratched into the walls the stories that confounded them. Paintings of animals in European caves were probably intended to have magical powers, and early peoples believed they were calling up spirits to help them. Classical Greeks documented details of curious cases. The difference is, perhaps, that in the past we sought to learn from the unexplained rather than set out to discount it.

A copy of The Life of St Columba, *who is said to have seen the Loch Ness Monster in the sixth century.*

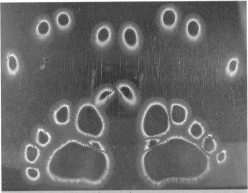

A Kirlian picture showing fingers and toes.

KIRLIAN PHOTOGRAPHY

Kirlian photography, sometimes called electrophotography, uses high-voltage electricity to produce an image. The technique was perfected in 1939 by Soviet electrician Semyon Kirlian. In a typical procedure the object being photographed is placed directly on an unexposed sheet of photographic film. In Kirlian photographs, objects appear to be surrounded by a glow or aura. In photographs of living objects this glow is quite pronounced, leading parapsychologists to claim that Kirlian photographs are evidence of the existence of 'psychic' energy.

A psychic reading letters and numbers while they are inside a sealed envelope – is this truth or trickery?

A NEW WORLD

SOME OF WHAT we now term 'unexplained' will one day be accepted as completely normal. Perhaps the beliefs of those who struggle to develop an understanding of the unknown and the paranormal will eventually take us to the brink of a new world. We may not grasp today what we can do with the knowledge of why, for example, some people have an ability to communicate with their minds alone, or how people suddenly combust or spontaneously heal, but by recognising that what we cannot explain is not necessarily trickery, superstition or simply madness, we can revolutionise our lives. This is not to say that all mysteries will have an explanation, or even that all of them are true. However, the one or two cases out of every thousand that are genuine can teach us a great deal about our world and what might lie outside it.

Unexplained phenomena are not new, nor have explanations been satisfactorily provided for age-old mysteries.

The aftermath of one of the most grisly of unexplained phenomena, spontaneous human combustion.

Unexplained Terms

aura: an invisible emanation produced by a person or object.

clairvoyance: the ability to perceive things beyond the reach of the normal human senses.

close encounters: sightings, contact or actual meetings made with alien beings or spacecraft. Close encounters of the first kind describe distant sightings, encounters of the third kind involve people meeting alien beings or entities.

cryptozoology: the search for animals who existance is unsubstantiated.

dowsing: the search for underground water using a forked rod or stick.

extra-sensory perception (ESP): the alleged ability to obtain information about the environment without using the five senses.

medium: a person used as a spiritual intermediary between the living and the dead.

out-of-body experience: in which a person experiences the sensation of floating outside of their own body.

paranormal: things that are beyond 'normal' explanations.

parapsychology: the study of mental phenomena that have no scientific explanation.

precognition: the alleged ability to forsee future events.

premonition: an intuitive feeling or vision of a future event.

prophecy: a message of truth about the future, usually religious in basis.

psychic: someone or something that is sensitive to para-psychological forces or influences not recognised by natural laws.

psychokinesis: the alteration of an object through the power of the mind alone.

reincarnation: the belief that on physical death of the body the soul is born again in another body.

telekinesis: the movement of an object caused by thought.

telepathy: the communication between people of thoughts or emotions through the mind alone.

teleportation: movement by means of telekinesis.

UFO: Unidentified Flying Object, usually used in reference to spaceships.

vortex: a swirling mass or motion of solid, liquid or gas that has the potential to be all-engulfing.

Adamski's account of his meeting with Venusians, first published in 1953.

STRANGE VANISHINGS

Introduction

THE PHENOMENON of unexplained disappearances is recorded in the earliest written works. Indeed, several examples of strange vanishings are mentioned by the Greek poet Homer in his epic poem *Iliad*, which was composed in the eighth century BC. The Bible's Old Testament contains more examples, including the miraculous departures from the world of the patriarch Enoch and the prophet Elijah.

DEFYING LOGIC

MANY OF THESE early disappearances can be considered allegorical, or the stuff of legends. More inexplicable are the vanishings that occurred in the twentieth century, when science and technology appear to have answers to most questions about unexplained phenomena. In most cases there are, eventually, explanations. But in a minority of cases, the disappearances defy logical explanation – such as the passenger liner *Waratah*, which was last seen off the coast of Africa in 1909. No wreckage or flotsam was ever found and her fate is unknown to this day.

All over the world individuals or groups of people have vanished and never been seen again. Sometimes ships are found floating intact upon the seas, but with no sign of captain or crew; sometimes aircraft with all their passengers vanish without trace of wreckage. Whether they occurred on land, at sea or in the air, these disappearances show that even in the scientific age there is still much in our world that eludes explanation.

The Greek poet Homer, one of the first to record examples of mysterious disappearances.

Missing Children

THE VAUGHAN CHILDREN

THIS IS ONE of the most peculiar disappearances on record, and to this day the case has never been satisfactorily resolved. In June 1906, the three children of a railway brakeman named Vaughan – his son aged 10 and his two daughters aged five and three – went to play in a large pasture field known as Forty Acres, a mile outside Gloucester. They played there regularly and had never come to any harm. On the day in question, the children did not return home for their tea and Mrs Vaughan went to look for them. There was no sign of them anywhere, and she instantly raised the alarm. A large search party consisting of policemen and volunteers was organised and for three days and nights, every inch of Forty Acres was searched. One of the search-party members, who later wrote about the case in his book *Mysteries Solved and Unsolved*, was Harold T. Wilkins. He said: 'We paid particular attention to the north-east corner of the field, where the pasture was bordered by tall, old elms, a thick hedge of thorn and bramble, and a deep ditch, separating it from a cornfield. Every inch was probed with sticks, and not a stone left unturned in the ditch. Had a dead dog been dumped there, he would certainly have been found. Not a trace of the missing children was found.'

LOST TIME

AFTER THREE DAYS, the search party was called off. It was decided that the missing children had been taken from the area and might never be seen alive again. And then, at 6 a.m. on the fourth day, a farm worker walking to work along the edge of the cornfield happened to look over the hedge and saw the three Vaughan children lying asleep in the ditch. The children were clean and didn't seem hungry, and they were amazed to hear that people had been looking for them. All they could remember was going to sleep in the ditch. For the rest of their lives, they claimed that they did not know what had happened for those three missing days. They all thought they had been to sleep for just a short time in the ditch and woken up later to the furore that had surrounded their disappearance.

Railwayman Vaughan's three children went missing without a trace; three days later they were found asleep and unharmed in a ditch.

Benjamin Bathurst, who mysteriously disappeared while carrying dispatches from Vienna.

Missing Men

BENJAMIN BATHURST

BATHURST WAS the third son of a bishop and a well-known and highly regarded diplomat. Early in 1809 he was sent to Vienna on a secret mission to the court of the Emperor Francis at a time of critical importance in the Napoleonic Wars. He was instrumental in mobilising the Austrian army against Napoleon, and as a result Bathurst believed that Napoleon was intent on revenge. He travelled as a merchant under the assumed name of Koch, and on 25 November he arrived at Perleberg, midway between Berlin and Hamburg, at a post-house. While the horses were being changed, he ordered some refreshment, and after his meal visited the local garrison. There he sought an interview with the commander Captain Klitzing, and informed him that he feared for his life. He asked for full protection and two soldiers remained with him until 7 o'clock that evening. He decided to travel on by night, which he believed would be safer, and arranged for the horses to be ready at nine. He stood outside the inn, watching his luggage being replaced in the carriage, and then stepped around to the head of the horses. He was never seen again. Without a word, a cry or any alarm, he had been spirited away.

Full searches went on for over a year, and the only sign of Bathurst was a pair of trousers found on 16 December in the local wood. The trousers were soaked with water and contained two bullet holes. One of the pockets revealed a note in Bathurst's handwriting, which stated that he feared danger from the Count d'Entraigues, a French double agent. Despite generous rewards being offered, no further clues came to light.

GLENN MILLER

THE FAMOUS BANDLEADER Glenn Miller disappeared on 15 December 1944. Along with other famous stars, Miller joined the USAAF and formed his famous American Air Force Band with the intention of entertaining the troops. In June 1944, they travelled to Britain to broadcast to the invasion forces. Regular BBC broadcasts were made and Miller planned a Christmas concert in Paris, which had returned to the Allies in August 1944. The band was due to be flown out from England in three USAAF transport aircraft, but bad weather delayed departure. Miller decided to go on ahead, and got a lift in a light aircraft – a 600 horsepower Norseman, on a non-operational flight to Bordeaux. On the morning of 15 December, the Norseman, piloted by Flying Officer John Morgan, took off from Abbots Ripton and made for the RAF airfield near Bedford to pick up Miller and his friend, Lt Colonel Norman Baessell, who had arranged the flight. The Norseman departed on the second leg of its journey at 1.55 p.m. and was never heard of again. The band followed on 18 December and were surprised that Miller was not there to meet them.

Band leader Glenn Miller, who disappeared during the Second World War.

The plane and its occupants were the subject of an intensive search, and despite rumours of crash landings, no wreckage was ever found, nor did communications with Paris and Britain ever show any problems while the plane was in the air.

Miller's plane took off for Bordeaux, but never reached its destination; no trace of it was ever found.

Missing Women

AMELIA EARHART

AMELIA MARY EARHART was the first woman to make a solo flight over the Atlantic Ocean. In July 1937 as she attempted the first round-the-world flight via the equator with navigator Frederick J. Noonan, her plane mysteriously disappeared after take-off from New Guinea. A massive search for Earhart and Noonan failed, and their fate became the subject of unending speculation. One theory is that their plane went down on the Pacific island of Nikumaroro, 800 km (500 miles) to the south of Howland Island, where she was to have landed. This theory was given more credibility in 1989 when an International Group for Historic Aviation Recovery announced that an expedition to the island had unearthed several artefacts, including a cigarette lighter and a pre-war aircraft battery. There was, however, no other sign of the wreckage, and certainly no bodies. Some

The aviator Amelia Earhart.

Newspaper report giving details of Earhart's last flight and the search that took place for her.

theorists believe that Amelia had been on a spying mission aimed at taking aerial photographs of Japanese military installations in the Marshall Islands and that she had been taken prisoner by the Japanese. Some weight was given to this theory in 1944 when Marshall islanders told the invading American Marines of two American flyers, a man and a woman, who had been taken by the Japanese seven years before. A photograph of Amelia was later found on the body of a dead Japanese soldier in Okinawa.

A contemporary female pioneer of the air, Jacqueline Cochronie, who claimed to possess psychic powers, suggested shortly after Amelia went missing that she and a badly injured Noonan were alive and afloat on the ditched aircraft for some time after the crash. Despite a four-million-dollar search lasting for two weeks, no sign of the craft or Earhart was ever found.

More than 200 men from the I/5th Norfolk regiment disappeared during an offensive in Gallipoli.

Missing Regiments

THE NORFOLK REGIMENT

IN 1915, over 200 men of the I/5th Norfolk regiment vanished from sight at Gallipoli in Turkey. The Gallipoli campaign of the First World War was undertaken by the Allies to relieve the pressure on the Russian Army in the Caucasus. The main battlefield of the campaign was the Suvla Plain. The Allies lay exposed on the plain where the Turks were hidden in the hills. The commander-in-chief, Sir Ian Hamilton, prepared the strategy, which was to carry out a mass assault on the Turks' entrenched positions.

On 12 August 1915, the British 163rd Brigade of Territorials was ordered forward to mop up any snipers in forward Turkish positions. The Brigade comprised the I/8th Hampshires, I/5th Suffolks, and I/4th and I/5th Norfolks, and they moved out in the late afternoon. The main body came under heavy fire and fell. However, the I/5th Norfolks on the right of the line of advance pressed on. Sir Ian Hamilton, in a report to Lord Kitchener, described what followed: 'At this stage many men were wounded or grew exhausted with thirst. These found their way back to camp during the night. But the Colonel [Beauchamp], with 16 officers and 250 men, still kept pushing forward, driving the enemy before him. Among these ardent souls was part of a fine company enlisted from the King's Sandringham Estates. Nothing more was seen or heard of any of them. They charged into the forest and were lost to sight or sound. None of them ever came back.'

Two hundred and sixty-seven men had

The soldiers, hot on the trail of the enemy, vanished into a forest and were never seen again.

vanished without trace. At the end of the war, the British pressed the Turks for their views on the matter, but they denied all knowledge of the Norfolks and were unable to produce any prisoners. Further enquiries led to the discovery of a number of bodies, crudely buried, but 140 men were still missing and never discovered. If they had been hit by enemy fire, their bodies would have fallen in quite a clearly defined area.

THE CHINESE ARMY

IN 1937, China and Japan had been at war for six months, and Japan was about to undertake one of the most horrific massacres in history – the 'rape of Nanking'. But events leading up to the massacre hold the secret of one of the most bizarre disappearances in history. South of the city, the Chinese Colonel Li Fu Sien decided to make a last-ditch stand in the low hills. Three thousand reinforcements were ordered, and the colonel set them up in a 3.2-km (2-mile) line close to an important bridge across the Yangtse River. They had a great deal of heavy artillery and were set to fight to the death. The colonel returned to his headquarters behind the line and waited for the Japanese to attack. At dawn he was awakened by an aide, who told him that they were unable to contact the soldiers at the line. They immediately set off to investigate and found that the positions were deserted. The guns were in position, but the men had vanished. There was no sign of fighting or trouble. The sentries on the bridge testified that no-one had crossed the bridge in the night. When the war was over, the Japanese had no record of the 3,000 missing men. They were never found.

Japanese troops during the war with China, in which 3,000 Chinese soldiers disappeared from their front-line posts with no sign of a struggle or bodies.

An Experiment with Time

J.W. DUNNE (1875–1949) was a British aviation pioneer, and enormously well regarded. In his famous book, *An Experiment with Time* (1927), Dunne described how he often had dreams about major disasters, only to find them later documented in the newspapers. He began to keep a dream diary, in which he maintained a highly detailed summary of each night's dream experiences.

J. W. Dunne concluded that as we sleep we are released from the linear time that we think of as reality.

He began to examine the dreams for possible evidence of future events, not just disasters or other major occurrences, but happenings of any magnitude. At the same time he kept a list of past events that appeared in the same dreams. After several months, he made a startling discovery, which was confirmed as time passed. He found that his dreams contained approximately the same number of past and future events.

LINEAR REALITY

HE CAME TO BELIEVE, based on this research, that in sleep we escape the linear, one-directional time that we think of as reality while awake. He compared time to a piano keyboard. When we're awake, we're sitting at the keyboard striking one note at a time, in sequence, from left to right. We cannot normally strike keys to the left ('the past') of the one in front of us, nor keys to the right ('the future'). But when we sleep, we are freed from the rigorous linearity.

Dunne's theory has been strongly criticised by many scientists, but it does offer an explanation for some of the strange disappearances that occur. Perhaps these people have jumped forward or backward in time? Time is like a record, and our human consciousness is like the record player's needle. Occasionally the needle can skip a groove, or even several grooves. Dunne's theory also offers an explanation for the strange glimpses of the future that provide such a challenge to parapsychologists.

Dunne compared his experiment with time to a piano keyboard, at which we sit, striking one key at a time, all the keys before the note we hit being the past, the ones after, the future.

MARINE MYSTERIES

Introduction

THERE IS NO question that seamen are amongst the most superstitious of us all, but does that explain the inordinate number of mysteries that surround ships and other vessels that travel on or under the sea and the aeroplanes that fly over it?

SECRETS OF THE OCEAN

DESPITE THE FACT that almost three-quarters of the globe is covered by water, we have charted just two per cent of the ocean floor. What lies within its depths may never be fully understood, but it would appear that the sea holds a strange power that has not yet been explained by science. One of the most frightening characteristics of the sea is its power to engulf large vessels completely, without any trace. Years-long searches into strange marine disappearances have been undertaken and have come up with nothing but a pocketful of useless and unproved theories. Unexplained vanishings at sea are more numerous and baffling than those on land. Furthermore, we may never fully comprehend this vast unknown.

The mysteries that the oceans hold are a source of endless fascination.

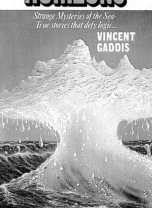

"FASCINATING"... Aurora Beacon-News

INVISIBLE HORIZONS

Strange Mysteries of the Sea—
True stories that defy logic...

VINCENT GADDIS

Cover of Vincent Gaddis's book Invisible Horizons, *about the secrets of the deep.*

THE POWER OF THE SEA

EVEN MORE frightening, perhaps, is the idea that triangles of sea can have a hypnotic or magnetic effect on aircraft and seacraft in its vicinity. The Bermuda Triangle and the Devil's Sea off Japan are two such examples. The huge number of vanishings and other phenomena in their midst have been classified 'natural', but other mysterious circumstances have yet to be explained by natural causes.

There are those who believe that the sea carries a great and almost living power. Can a powerful marine tragedy create ghost ships? Can people really disappear on the sea, with no sign of wreckage, bodies or attempts to flee a sinking ship? Although the likelihood is that one day we will find rational explanations for these occurrences, for now they remain a mystery.

The *Mary Celeste*

IN NOVEMBER 1872, Captain Benjamin Spooner Briggs set sail with his wife and two-year-old daughter and a crew of seven aboard the cargo ship *Mary Celeste*. They left New York on their way to Genoa with a cargo of crude (unconsumable) alcohol aboard, and passed through good weather before meeting a 'moderate gale' around the Azores.

Also sailing from New York was the *Dei Gratia*, a British ship heading for Gibraltar. On 5 December, the crew spotted the *Mary Celeste*. It appeared to be in trouble, and upon drawing closer they found that the wheel was unattended. Three seaman were sent aboard to investigate, but they found the ship deserted. The cargo was intact, as were the food supplies, and the crew's clothing was on board. The ship's log had been filled in regularly until the last entry on 25 November, which suggested that the ship had been empty for up to 10 days. A small sailboat, a chronometer and a sextant were missing, but apart from a little storm damage to the sails and rigging, the ship was in good order and there was so sign of any untoward activity on the boat.

Benjamin Spooner Briggs, captain of the cargo ship Mary Celeste.

WHAT HAPPENED?

TO THIS DAY the answer is unknown. Various theories have been put forward, including murder of the captain by the crew, voluntary abandonment by the crew, pirates and even an attack by a sea monster, but none has been proved, despite over 100 years of investigation. One of the most widely accepted explanations is based on the work of Dr Richard McIver, who believes that deposits of methane gases are held under the oceans. When the gas is released, it bubbles up to the surface. If the boats do not sink before the gas disperses, they ride back up to the surface. Perhaps this occurred on the night of 25 November 1872, causing the crew to panic. They may have abandoned ship and been sucked down by the gas, while the *Mary Celeste* stayed afloat.

The Mary Celeste *as it was encountered by the crew of the* Dei Gratia; *they found it completely deserted.*

The Bermuda Triangle

An old map showing the area that was believed to be covered by the Bermuda Triangle. Ships and aircraft have been known to disappear here.

THE BERMUDA TRIANGLE, also called the Devil's Triangle, is an area of the Atlantic Ocean off south-east Florida, where the disappearance of ships and aeroplanes has, on a number of occasions, led to speculation about inexplicable turbulence and other atmospheric disturbances. Violent storms and downward air currents frequently occur there, but studies have failed to reveal any significant peculiarities about the area in question. Today, boundaries of the Bermuda Triangle have been formed by drawing an imaginary line from Melbourne in Florida, to Bermuda, to Puerto Rico, and back to Florida.

AIR TROUBLE

MANY PLANES have disappeared or experienced inexplicable navigation equipment failure while in the Bermuda Triangle. Key cases include:

- In 1928, Charles Lindbergh reported both his compasses failing and the presence of a 'heavy haze' obscuring vision, while on a flight from Havana to Florida.
- In 1948, a DC3 private charter plane carrying 32 passengers plus crew disappeared.
- In March 1950, an American Globemaster disappeared on the northern edge of the triangle en route to Ireland.
- In 1954, a Navy Lockheed Super Constellation vanished with 42 people on board.
- In 1962, an Air Force tanker KB150 flying from Virginia to the Azores disappeared.
- In 1965, a C1119 flying Boxcar with 10 aboard was lost in the south-east Bahamas.
- In 1968, Jim Blocker reported radio and navigational failure inside a bank of clouds while flying from Nassau to Palm Beach.

The Bermuda Triangle has proved one of the most popular mysteries of modern times.

FLIGHT 19

ON 5 DECEMBER 1945, five Avenger torpedo bombers took off from a US Navy base at Fort Lauderdale, Florida, for target practice off the coast. After the first run they regrouped, but inexplicably failed to recognise their surroundings. Lt Charles Taylor radioed base saying, 'We seem to be lost ... everything is wrong, strange ... We can't be sure of any direction ... even the ocean doesn't look as it should'. Confused scraps of conversation between the crew hinted at malfunctioning compasses, high winds and low fuel. Despite a massive search by nearly 100 ships and several submarines, no wreckage or bodies were ever found.

EYE-WITNESS REPORT

ON 11 JUNE 1986, Martin Caidin and his crew were flying from Bermuda to Jacksonville Naval Air Station in Florida, equipped with a great deal of

Martin Caidin and his crew managed to fly through the Bermuda Triangle, but within the area all their avionic equipment ceased working.

navigational equipment. The craft received satellite photographs of the area in which they were flying, and it was a clear, bright day with no sign of poor weather. Without warning, Caidin was unable to see the outer portion of his left wing, and then the right wing. According to their readouts, there should not have been any mist. Around him the blue sky changed to yellow and they were in what he later described as a 'creamy yellow version of a whiteout', with the instruments 'going crazy'. He said 'two million dollars of avionics just up and died'. Caidin was able

Five Avenger torpedo bombers that were setting off for target practice disappeared without a trace within the Bermuda Triangle in 1945.

to see a tunnel-like hole above the plane, where he could see blue sky, and another hole running down to the sea visible below. They stayed calm and managed to guide the plane through the mist for four hours. When they finally reached clear air again, they looked back to see what had caused the problems and saw only clear sky for miles on end. Their equipment began to work again and the plane landed without incident.

NAVAL MYSTERIES

THERE ARE more than 30 recorded disappearances relating to sea vessels in the Bermuda Triangle area. Some of these include:

- In 1840, the French ship *Rosalie* was found on course to Havana from Europe in the Triangle area, with sails set, cargo intact and all hands missing.
- In January 1880, the British frigate *Atlanta* left Bermuda for England with 290 aboard. She vanished without trace.
- In 1924, the *Raifuku Maru*, a Japanese freighter, radioed for help between the Bahamas and Cuba before disappearing.
- In 1938, an Anglo-Australian freighter with a crew of 39 disappeared. The last message was received west of Azores. It read 'All well'.
- In 1963, the *Marine Sulphur Queen*, a 130-m (425-ft) freighter, vanished without message, clues or debris en route to Norfolk, Virginia, from Texas.
- In 1970, the freighter *Milton Latrides*, en route from New Orleans to Cape Town, disappeared.
- In 1984, the 27-m (88-ft) brig *Marques* was lost on the northern border of the Triangle. Eighteen were missing.

WHAT HAPPENED?

THERE HAVE been many theories surrounding the incidents that have occurred in the Bermuda Triangle. One popular notion is that the Triangle is an ideal place for aliens to abduct humans. Another theory links the Triangle with Atlantis, suggesting that the legendary lost civilisation existed in the area, and that its magnetic or gravitational forces continued to exist long after the city sank beneath the waves.

One theory is that ships in the Bermuda Triangle were capsized by giant waves.

Others suggest that planes and ships are affected by some type of magnetic-field disturbance which may exist in the Bermuda Triangle. More straightforward is the idea that the ships and planes lost went down for conventional reasons – mechanical failure, pilot error, fuel loss or even blistering heat. However, no wreckage from any of the missing planes or ships has been found, and there is still no explanation for the equipment failure and whiteouts which appear to occur there.

Others suggest that whirlpools may be responsible for the disappearance of vessels in the Triangle.

The *Dawn* and the
Island Queen

IN THE 1930s, a 75-ton schooner named *Dawn* set sail from Alabama heading for Barbados. It was commanded by Captain Reg Mitchell, a very experienced seaman who knew the route and the area well, and carried a crew of eight. Despite continuing fair weather, the ship went missing and failed to arrive at its destination. A look-out for it was kept by Captain

Mitchell's fellow skippers and by aircraft flying over the area. There was no sign of the ship or its crew. Yet three months later, the ship turned up again, adrift a few miles off the Mexican coast. They found the *Dawn* to be in excellent condition: the sails were neatly furled, the engine was in good running order, and the diesel tanks were more than half full. But there was no sign of Captain Mitchell and his crew members. To this day nobody knows what became of them.

WITHOUT A TRACE

ON 5 AUGUST 1944, a 75-ton schooner *Island Queen* set sail from the port of St George's in Grenada. Aboard the vessel were its crew, consisting of the experienced Captain Salhab and 10 seamen, and 57 passengers. The latter were mainly tourists who were travelling to the island of St Vincent to take part in a holiday festival there. The journey was some 120 km (75 miles) and would take a night to complete. En route, the *Island Queen* was passed by another boat, the *Providence Mark*, and all seemed to be well. When the schooner failed to reach its destination, an air search was begun, and the British Fleet Air Arm and the US Navy department became involved. The search went on for several days without result. No survivors were picked up. No bodies were discovered afloat nor were any washed ashore. No wreckage was found. No oil patches were sighted on the surface of the sea. The ship had vanished completely, with 68 people on board. No clue has since been found to suggest what took place on that clear night.

The Cyclops, *a British Navy ship that disappeared without trace en route to the West Indies in 1918.*

The *Titanic*

THE LOSS OF the *Titanic* was undoubtedly the most tragic accident in marine history, and although conspiracy theories abound, there is no doubt that her sinking was the result of a collision with an iceberg. What is interesting, however, is the fact that the sinking of the *Titanic* was the subject of numerous prophecies.

Several days into her first voyage, *Titanic* struck an unseen iceberg and sank, taking 1,500 passengers and crew to their deaths. The tragedy of the sinking lay in the fact that the owners of the ship, who had been utterly convinced that she was 'unsinkable', had failed to provide enough lifeboats.

Titanic striking the iceberg that resulted in its destruction, and the deaths of 1,500 people.

There are at least 20 known cases of people who had premonitions of disaster before the ship sailed. In fact, the theory of precognition (the ability to see things before they happen) gained international credence following the accident. Some passengers refused to board the ship; others had relatives among the passengers and warned them in advance, or sensed disaster.

PROPHECIES OF DOOM

WILLIAM STEAD, a well-known newspaperman, was warned in writing by a psychic that he would be in great danger during April 1912, and that he should avoid water and travel at the same time. He ignored the warning and died in the disaster. Ironically, Stead had written an article noting that just such an accident could occur.

Retired seaman Morgan Robertson was a struggling writer when, in 1898, he had a vision in which he saw a huge liner collide with an iceberg. He remembered hearing the words 'April' and 'unsinkable'. Inspired by this vision, he wrote the story *The Wreck of the Titan*, in which a near-identical ship to the *Titanic*, the *SS Titan*, sinks on her maiden voyage after striking an iceberg, with hundreds perishing because of an inadequate number of lifeboats.

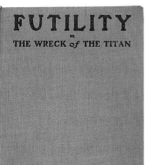

Morgan Robertson's book The Wreck of the Titan *describes events too similar to those of the* Titanic *to be coincidence – the book was written 14 years before the event.*

The *Flying Dutchman*

T HE *FLYING DUTCHMAN* is probably the most celebrated ghost ship, dating from the seventeenth century when Captain Hendrik van der Decken, rounding the Cape of Good Hope, encountered such unfavourable weather that he had difficulty progressing. He refused the pleas of passengers and crew to seek a port until the storm abated, and stubbornly fought to round the Cape. He swore that he would round the 'damned' Cape if it took until Doomsday.

GHOST-SHIP SIGHTINGS

THE *FLYING DUTCHMAN* sank with only one or two survivors, but a ghostly replica of the ship has reportedly been seen in the area by many experienced and reliable sailors, and this is a phantom that has some official recognition: records of sightings are preserved in the files of the British Admiralty. Among the alleged sightings are those that took place in 1823, 1835, 1881, 1890, 1893, 1905, 1911, 1916, 1923, 1939 and 1942. Among the witnesses are King George V, when he was a naval cadet, together with 12 other witnesses including his brother Prince Clarence, then heir to the throne. During the Second World War Admiral Karl Doenitz, Hitler's commander-in-chief of U-boats, reported sighting the *Flying Dutchman*: 'Certain of my U-boat crews claimed they saw the *Flying Dutchman* or some other so-called phantom ship on their tours of duty east of Suez. When they returned to their base, the men said they preferred facing the combined strength of Allied warships in the North Atlantic than know the terror a second time of being confronted by a phantom vessel.'

The phantom ship Flying Dutchman.

ANIMAL MYSTERIES

Introduction

CRYPTOZOOLOGY IS, according to its founder Belgian biologist Bernard Heuvelmans, 'not an arcane or occult zoology'. It comes from the Greek words *kryptos* ('hidden') and *logos* ('discourse'). Heuvelmans explains that such 'animals' (often deemed monsters) are typically 'known to a local population – at least sufficiently so that we often indirectly know of their existence and certain aspects of their appearance and behaviour. It would be better to call them animals undescribed by science'.

According to the founding meeting of the International Society of Cryptozoology, held in 1982, 'what makes an animal of interest to cryptozoology is that it is unexpected'.

WEIRD CREATURES

WHAT FALLS into the brief of a cryptozoologist? Many would consider it to be the stuff of nightmares – phantom animals, known varieties of animals in unbelievable or impossible locations, sea and lake monsters, ape-men, giant squid, sea serpents and the Yeti.

An alleged sea monster photographed in Stonehaven Bay, Hook Island, Australia.

The Australian man-beast, known as the Yowie.

Many of the most intensive cryptozoological investigations have been unsuccessful, leading many mainstream scientists to dismiss the discipline as illegitimate. But how can we explain the well-documented, amazingly similar accounts of animals or monsters appearing in unexpected places? While science might speculate that these animals simply cannot exist, evidence suggests that they may – outside the imaginations of witnesses, many of whom are unwilling and highly reputable.

The debate is, however, irrelevant in the long term, for first-hand accounts continue to pile up. Some sightings have been captured using the tools of modern-day technology, including photographs and films. In some cases we have to rely on the integrity of the multiple witnesses. But as long as there are witness accounts, the search for the planet's most mysterious and elusive creatures will continue.

The Monster of Chesapeake Bay

CHESSIE, AS IT has come to be known, is the frequently sighted creature of the Chesapeake Bay area in the eastern United States. The creature has been sighted regularly since the nineteenth century, and is described as being a long, dark, serpent-like animal. In 1982, the American Robert Frew filmed Chessie from a house on Kent Island, which overlooks the bay. Frew and his wife spotted the creature in shallow, clear water about 200 m (700 ft) from the house. He videotaped the creature as it swam towards a group of swimmers. It dived beneath the swimmers and reappeared on the other side of them. The creature they caught on film was around 9 m (30 ft) in length, and about 30 cm (1 ft) in diameter. It was dark brown with a humped back.

SIGHTINGS OF CHESSIE

IN 1978, a retired CIA employee, Donald Kyker, reported seeing Chessie and three other sea monsters about 70 m (230 ft) offshore. His neighbours also witnessed the animals, and they provided descriptions of 9-m (30-ft) long, sleek, dark-grey creatures swimming at about 10 kph (6 mph).

Sightings of Chessie have remained consistent over the years and occur most frequently between May and September. The area is more heavily populated during this period, which could explain the increased sightings, but it is also possible that the creature migrates during this time. The witness list includes members of the coastguard and naval officers, airline

pilots, an ex-CIA official and an FBI agent. The photos and
film that exist of Chessie were studied by Smithsonian officials
and they concluded that it was a living animal that was
pictured, but they could not identify it.

*Sea or lake monsters remain the subject of speculation as sightings and
photographs are inconclusive. This sea monster was seen from the* Daedalus
when in the South Atlantic in 1848.

The Loch Ness Monster

THE LOCH NESS MONSTER, or 'Nessie', has an almost mythical status. It is said that in AD 565, when the Irish priest who became St Columba went to Scotland to convert the Picts to Christianity, the monster threatened a follower of St Columba. The priest made the sign of the cross and thwarted the beast. Sightings of Nessie have been reported regularly over the years since that time, although some sightings have proved to be hoaxes or honest mistakes. The likelihood of a creature of that size living in the lake is small, but not impossible. Interesting photographs have been taken and a great deal of supportive data indicates that something does exist in the lake. However, sophisticated sonar equipment has been used to try and track Nessie and little evidence has

been provided to show that a monster really does live in the loch. Numerous separate serious investigations have been conducted, but no physical evidence has been found. However, since the 1930s more than 3,000 separate sightings have been reported and studied by experts.

A photograph believed to be of Nessie, taken from nearby Urquhart Castle.

'Operation Deepscan', using sonar boats – one of the attempts to find out exactly what lurks in the deep waters of Loch Ness.

SIGHTINGS OF NESSIE

ONE OF the most detailed sightings occurred in 1933. Mrs John Mackay was being driven along the new road, which gave a perfect view of the lake. She said: 'I couldn't believe what we were seeing. I have never seen such an enormous thing. It was just an enormous black body, going up and down. You could not put a name to it. It could have been an elephant or a whale.' Two of the strongest pieces of evidence to support the existence of Nessie were put through stringent scientific analysis. They were two cine films, far more difficult to fake than still photographs, and they seemed to show an animal speeding through the water and then submerging. Experts assessed that the animal was more than 2 m (7 ft) long, and moved at around 15 kph (10 mph). Positive identification, however, has remained impossible.

Ogopogo

THE BEST-KNOWN Canadian lake monster is Ogopogo. In 1926, Roy W. Brown, editor of the *Vancouver Sun*, wrote: 'Too many reputable people have seen [the monster] to ignore the seriousness of actual facts.' Archival records of Ogopogo's existence date back to 1872 and sightings continue to be reported to the present day.

Ogopogo is most often described as being approximately 30–60 cm (1–2 ft) in diameter, and 4.5–6 m (15–20 ft) in length. He has been seen repeatedly across the years in Lake Okanagan, and some witnesses claim that they have seen him on land. Unusual footprints have been found by the lake, which give credence to the view that the monster may be partly reptilian. His head has been described variously as horse- or goat-like, and many witnesses claim that the monster is log-shaped.

Lake Okanagan in Canada, where many sightings of the lake monster Ogopogo have been reported.

A Basilosaurus – many think Ogopogo may be a form of this primitive serpentine whale.

SCIENTIFIC INVESTIGATIONS

CRYPTOZOOLOGIST Roy P. Mackal believes that there is a small population of aquatic fish-eating animals residing in Lake Okanagan. Mackal initially assumed that the type of animal in Lake Okanagan was the same creature that he believed was in Loch Ness, but after a careful examination of the available data, he determined that the Canadian creature may be a form of primitive whale: *Basilosaurus cetoides*. He notes that the general appearance of *Basilosaurus* tallies almost exactly with the log-like descriptions of Ogopogo.

While Ogopogo has never attained the fame of the Loch Ness Monster, the creature of Lake Okanagan has regularly caused quite a stir in the international press. Monster hunters from all over the world have been drawn to the area for research purposes, and multiple witness sightings of Ogopogo, so rare with many other controversial phenomena, have occurred on many occasions.

The Yeti

THE YETI, or the Abominable Snowman, has been regularly sighted in the Himalayan mountains for hundreds of years. According to legend and eyewitness reports, the creature is tall and manlike, covered with shaggy hair. Accounts say that it ranges between 2 and 3 m (6 to 9 ft) in height and has a conical scalp, pointed ears, a hairless chest and a human-like face. The creature is said to be aggressive, and will attack anyone who ventures close enough. The descriptions are quite similar to those of Bigfoot (see page 70).

SIGHTINGS OF THE YETI

IN 1832, the British explorer B. H. Hodgson travelled to the Himalayas to record the lifestyle of the Nepalese. In one letter home he told how the tribespeople lived in fear of a mysterious, tall, erect creature covered in thick black hair. Men like Eric Shipton, the Everest pioneer, and Lord Hunt, leader of the first successful assault on Everest, have also been convinced that the Yeti exists. Don Whillans, a famous British climber, was on

An illustration of the Yeti, sighted in the Himalayan mountains.

The Russian man-beast hunter Igor Bourtsev, holding a cast of a man-beast footprint.

Annapurna in 1970 when, by the light of the moon, he watched an ape-like creature cavort in the snow for about 20 minutes. The next day he saw distinctive and inexplicable tracks.

But the most intriguing evidence relating to the Yeti is the photographs of footprints in the snow. There are at least two dozen photographs of footprints taken by mountaineers, but no photographs of the Yeti itself are known to exist.

Eric Shipton's 1951 picture, taken in the Menlung Basin in Nepal, is clear and precise. When Lord Hunt took his 1978 pictures of tracks 35 m (14 in) long and 17.5 cm (7 in) wide, he noticed that the animal was so heavy that it had broken through snow on which he could safely walk.

OTHER MAN-BEASTS

Similar creatures to the Yeti have been spotted all over the world, including Russia, where they are known as 'Almas', Australia, where they are called 'Yowies', and not forgetting the better-known American Bigfoot or Sasquatch and the Chinese Wildman.

Bigfoot

ACCORDING TO the Native Americans of the United States and Canada, there is a manlike beast of no known species, about 2.5 m (8 ft) tall, with a broad chest and shoulders but virtually no neck. It was known by the Native Americans as Sasquatch, later named 'Bigfoot' by settlers. In the nineteenth century, explorer David Thomas discovered evidence of the strange animal, in the shape of footprints, which were at least 35 cm (14 in) long, near Jasper, Alberta.

Sightings continued across the years, but they gained ultimate credibility in 1903 when President Theodore Roosevelt recounted the story of two trappers in Idaho who were attacked by a mysterious creature. In 1924, Albert Ostman, a lumberman from Langley, British Columbia, claims to have been attacked by a giant Bigfoot. He said the beast was about 2.5m (8 ft) tall. The creature picked up

The famous film of Bigfoot taken by Roger Patterson at Bluff Creek, Northern California in 1967.

Roger Patterson, holding casts made from the footprints of Bigfoot within hours of taking his film.

Ostman, still in his sleeping bag, and carried him 'like a sack of potatoes' for three hours. He was kept in the lair of the Bigfoot, where other males and females also lived, for almost a week. He finally escaped, and his description of the creatures matched exactly the accounts of Bigfoot.

FACING BIGFOOT

ON 20 OCTOBER 1967, Roger Patterson, a former rancher, was tracking through the forests around Bluff Creek in Northern California with a Native American friend when they emerged into a clearing and came face to face with a Bigfoot. Patterson shot an amazing 9 m (29 ft) of colour film as it loped across his field of vision. They also took casts of the footprints left by the creature. The film was shown worldwide and most experts believed it to be genuine.

Leading authority Dr Napier wrote: 'The North American Bigfoot or Sasquatch has a lot going for it. Too many claim to have seen it, or at least to have seen footprints, to dismiss its reality out of hand.'

The Chinese Wildman

IN CHINA, TOO, there are legends of a wildman, or 'yeren'. Information collected over the years suggests that there are two types of yeren, one of about 1 m (3 ft) in height and another of perhaps 2 m (7 ft), and two types of footprint have been documented, which lend credence to this belief, the larger one bearing similarities to that of a man, only 30 to 40 cm (12 to 16 in) in length, the smaller one more like that of an ape, roughly 20 cm (8 in) long. The yeren share the characteristics of other man-beasts from around the world, with their ape-like features and hairy bodies.

INVESTIGATING THE WILDMAN

IN THE 1980s, a party led by Gene Poirier, professor of anthropology at Ohio State University, collected a number of hair samples. These had been found by farmers working in some of the most remote regions of central China. At Ohio, and at Birmingham University in the UK, researchers used special microscopes to establish that the hairs contained 54 times more zinc and iron than human hairs and eight times as much as animal hairs. Professor Poirier, an avowed sceptic of man-beasts, declared: 'We have established that the animal does not fall into any known category. This is the first evidence of the existence of a higher primate.'

Close-up of a hair believed to be from a man-beast; analysis of such hairs has proved that they are unlikely to be from a human or any known animal.

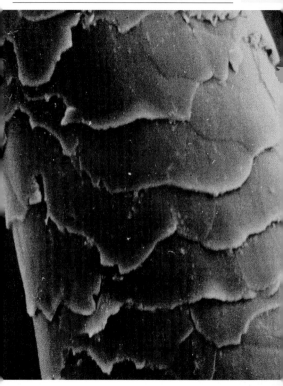

ALIEN ENCOUNTERS

Introduction

AROUND THE WORLD, thousands of people claim that they have been abducted by aliens. Many more claim to have witnessed some sort of extra-terrestrial activity, in the form of a UFO or an alien. Many of these claims seem ludicrous, but a small minority cannot be explained away: the witnesses are reliable, all modern investigative methods have shown that they are telling the truth, and the reports are confirmed by – and remarkably similar (even identical) to – accounts from other witnesses.

A 1952 illustration of Kenneth Arnold's sighting of nine UFOs over Mount Rainier in the Cascade Mountains.

STRANGE SIGHTINGS IN SPACE

IT IS GENERALLY accepted that the modern age of the UFO began with Kenneth Arnold's sighting of nine strange objects in the air over the Cascade Mountains, Washington, on 24 June 1947. In the decades since then, there have been hundreds of thousands of reports from all around the world of UFOs, alien contact experiences and abductions, and the result has been a widespread interest and indeed industry built up around the phenomenon.

But are aliens a modern mystery? The folklore and legends of many cultures show that there are striking correlations between their beliefs and records, and the numerous modern reports of alien encounters, implying that human interaction with the inhabitants of other worlds might have been taking place throughout history.

The COMING
of the SAUCERS

$2.50

By Kenneth Arnold & Ray Palmer

The cover of Arnold's book, in which he describes his UFO sightings in 1947.

The Philadelphia Experiment

IN 1943, the US Navy is alleged to have undertaken a series of top-secret experiments into invisibility. The story first surfaced in January 1956, following the publication of a book by Morris Jessup entitled *The Case for the UFO*. In the book he appealed for research into Albert Einstein's unified field theory. In response, he received two letters from someone calling himself Carlos Allende (later just Carl Allen).

THE INVISIBLE SHIP

ALLEN CLAIMED that he had been serving on a US ship in 1943 and had witnessed an experiment that made a destroyer completely invisible. He provided a great deal of detail and suggested that on the basis of the horrific effects of this experiment, all future research should be stopped. The ship in question, the USS *Eldridge*, not only became invisible to radar, but it became invisible to the naked eye as well. It was, according to Allen, teleported from a dockyard in Philadelphia to the Navy Yard at Norfolk, Virginia, several hundred miles away. But the consequences were terrible. When the ship reappeared in the Philadelphia yard, several crew members had become fused with the decks and the bulkheads of the ship, while the rest had been driven mad. Some crewmen subsequently burst into flames spontaneously, and other survivors babbled about encountering strange alien beings.

When Jessup began to investigate the affair, the Navy asked him if he would be interested in working on a similar project.

He declined, and in 1959 was found dead in his car, asphyxiated by exhaust gas. Some believe that he was killed before he could publicise the effects of the Philadelphia Experiment.

Although the whole story is more than likely to be a hoax, it has certainly caught the imagination of the public.

A still from the film The Philadelphia Experiment, *inspired by the unsolved case of the mysterious invisible US Navy destroyer.*

THE MYSTERIOUS UNKNOWN

IN *THE MYSTERIOUS UNKNOWN*, Robert Charroux cites another version of the experiment, as reported from the former USSR. The Soviets believed that the US Navy was investigating a magnetic version of the Möbius strip. This strip is a one-sided ring of paper, formed by taking a long strip of paper, giving one of its ends a half twist and then gluing the two ends of the strip together to form a ring. If the circle is cut along the centre of the strip, all the way around, the strip unfolds into one large ring instead of two interlinked rings as expected. In the Soviet version of the experiment, the vessel was a submarine, and the Möbius strip consisted of a powerful magnetic field. As the submarine pursued its course around the magnetic strip, turning over in the course of each revolution, an electronic device was used to cut the field in two. At this point, the submarine vanished, appearing miles away. As in the American version, the Soviets claimed that some of the crew died and others became insane.

Although the tale of the Philadelphia Experiment is most likely an elaborate hoax, many theories and explanations have been put forward.

AN UNSOLVED MYSTERY

WHATEVER THE CASE, both versions are based on the use of a magnetic field of unusual power. In 1979, Charles Berlitz and William Moore published an investigation, after tracking down Carl Allen. They established only limited evidence that something strange had occurred, but the steadfast silence from the US Navy about the experiment, and the wealth of detail supplied by Allen and another seaman who later came forward, make this one of the most bizarre and unsolved mysteries of the twentieth century.

UFO contactee George Adamski (left).

The Venus Creature

GEORGE ADAMSKI was a Polish-American who ran a hamburger stand in the vicinity of the Mount Palomar Observatory, California. In 1953, he claimed that he had been in contact with extraterrestrial visitors since 1946. His landmark contact came on 20 November 1952, after he and six other people drove into the desert to see if they could spot and photograph a UFO. Before long they sighted a cigar-shaped UFO and Adamski took a number of photographs. He wandered down the road, where he suddenly saw a figure waving at him. When he approached, he saw that the man was tall and blond, wearing a one-piece suit, with a broad belt around his waist.

COMMUNICATING WITH ALIENS

A SMALL UFO stood some distance away. Adamski moved to shake hands, but the tall stranger insisted on a palm-to-palm greeting. He indicated that he was from Venus (after Adamski asked a series of questions). After this first encounter, Adamski claimed to have been contacted quite frequently, although not always face-to-face. The aliens were apparently telepathic and could contact him at any time.

Their message was simple: atomic tests carried out on Earth were producing dangerous fallout, which was threatening other planets in the solar system. He claimed that they must be stopped.

Adamski later made further claims, detailing other contacts with extra-terrestrials in his book *Inside the Spaceships*. He claimed that he had been invited to board ships. He noted that cigar-shaped UFOs were 'mother ships' and vehicles we know as flying saucers were 'scout ships'.

Adamski gave detailed descriptions of other planets, from his own knowledge or from the aliens, which caused great excitement among many believers.

Adamski is now generally regarded as a fraud, but his film footage of UFOs continues to perplex scientists, who can find nothing to suggest that it was fabricated.

Adamski's account of his meeting with Venusians, first published in 1953.

The Green Children

A STORY DATING from the middle of the twelfth century revolves around two green children, who were found weeping and wandering in a field. They were taken to the nearest village, Woolpit in Suffolk, and held in captivity at the home of Sir Richard de Calne.

According to William of Newburgh, the children were dressed in 'garments of strange colour and unknown materials'. They spoke no English and refused all food offered to them, apart from green beans. The children were baptised and the boy sickened and died. The girl learned to eat other foods and soon lost her green colouring. Over time, she was able to communicate in English and she 'asserted that the inhabitants, and all that they had in that country, were of a green colour; and that they saw no sun, but enjoyed a degree of light like what is after sunset. Being asked how she came into this country with the aforesaid boy, she replied that as they were following their flocks they came to a certain cavern, until they came to its mouth. When they came out of it, they were struck senseless by the excessive light of the sun, and the unusual temperature of the air; and they thus lay for a long time. Being terrified by the noise of those who came on them, they wished to fly, but could not find the entrance of the cavern before they were caught'.

A MYSTERY SOLVED?

WERE THESE children really beings from another time and place? or could there be a rational explanation for their existence? The simplest answer is that they strayed to Woolpit from their own home, far away. Researchers have made

suggestions based on the information provided by the children.
It is probable that the story grew with re-telling, so that today it is
part fact, part fairy tale, and the mystery is unlikely to be solved.

*Village sign depicting the Green Children, who have become local legends
in the village of Woolpit in Suffolk.*

Betty and Barney Hill

IN SEPTEMBER 1961, Betty and Barney Hill were driving from Canada to New Hampshire when they saw a bright object like a star descending through the sky. Barney Hill examined it with binoculars and concluded that it looked like a spacecraft or a satellite. The family dog became nervous and restless in the back of the car and they stopped to let him out, with the strange craft still in full view. The couple drove on, and began to feel drowsy. They woke up an hour later, with no memory of what had happened in the interim. They had not only lost an hour, but they were some 56 km (35 miles) further into their journey.

Artist's impression of Betty and Barney Hill's UFO encounter.

PROOF FROM HYPNOSIS?

Betty and Barney Hill, who claim to have been abducted by aliens in 1961.

AFTER THE experience, the Hills suffered from nightmares and were concerned that they might have experienced some sort of breakdown. They consulted a series of doctors and Dr Benjamin Simons, a neurosurgeon, helped them to recall what had happened by hypnotising them individually. Their stories under hypnosis were the same: the engine of their car had failed upon the approach of a UFO; they had been taken on board the UFO and given a full medical examination by creatures that were not human; they were then returned to their car, further along the road.

PLANETARY EFFECTS

It has since emerged that an anomalous radar contact was detected in the area of their sighting on the night in question, at a time (2.14 a.m.) that could tie in with the Hills' encounter. But there are other, less otherworldly explanations. One of the hypnotists concluded that the Hills could have simply recalled a dream, rather than an actual event, under hypnosis. Also, it was later realised that the star and the spaceship that they had reported in the sky were most likely to be the planets Saturn and Jupiter, which were both clearly visible on that evening.

Aliens?

THE LIVINGSTON ENCOUNTER

ON 9 NOVEMBER 1979, Bob Taylor, a 60-year-old Scottish forestry foreman, widely regarded as being 'sensible and straightforward', was at work at Livingston, near the M8 Glasgow-Edinburgh motorway.

He encountered a silver-coloured domed spacecraft in a clearing, and two objects shaped like sea-mines, each with six spikes, peeled off the craft and came towards him. They grabbed him by the sides of his trousers and tore them, leaving scratch marks on his thighs.

An interpretation of Bob Taylor's encounter with alien spacecraft in Livingston, Scotland.

Taylor then fainted, although he vaguely recalls being dragged towards the craft. When he woke, the creatures and craft had disappeared, but trailmarks of dragging feet were later found. There were also a dozen deep triangular marks in the ground, two parallel tracks and flattened grass.

MYSTERY AT ROSWELL

IN 1995, British ufologists unveiled an old film showing US scientists examining the corpse of an alien. It has been linked to a reported UFO crash near Roswell, USA, in 1947. In July of that year, a press release was issued from Roswell Army Air Field in New Mexico, which stated: 'The many rumours regarding the Flying Disc became a reality yesterday when the Intelligence

Office of the 509th Bomb Group of the Eighth Air Force, Roswell Army Air Field, was fortunate enough to gain possession of a disc ...'.

Within 24 hours of this press release, a cover story about a weather balloon had been deployed. There was dispute about this, however. The Intelligence Officer of the 509th Bomb Group, Major Jesse Marcel, had witnessed the strange wreckage, and claimed it was not a weather balloon.

EXPLAINING THE MYSTERY

RECENT INVESTIGATIONS have revealed that the military were indeed undertaking some experiments at the time using metal foil balloons and this seems the most likely explanation for what was found at Roswell. The alien autopsy film has never been verified as authentic and although there were witnesses who claim to have seen some alien beings, their descriptions do not fit that of the alien in the film. The whole truth may never be known.

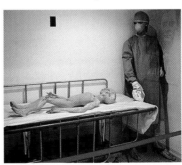

A display at the Roswell Museum in New Mexico, showing an autopsy of an alleged dead alien.

CURSES AND JINXES

Introduction

THERE IS NO question that some people – or even animals or vehicles – attract more than their share of tragedy. These cases are immediately considered to be the victim of a curse, a 'hex' or a jinx. In other words, people are all too willing to believe that fate, religion or even the occult can control events on Earth. But how much can be attributed to bad luck or coincidence? And how many events occur because the people involved believe in curses?

A handwritten late-eighteenth century curse, which was found with a curse doll.

An Australian aboriginal pointing bone, used to place curses.

TRAGIC AURAS

SOME EXPERTS believe that tragedy can create a 'negative thought field', which predisposed people tune into. In other words, if a tragic event has occurred, a sort of tragic aura is left behind. When people are frightened, nervous or even simply sensitive, they can be affected by this aura in a negative way.

Similarly, when individuals who have been cursed as the result of non-Western or primitive rituals die, it is believed to be because of the victim's belief in the power of the curse. Dr Herbert Basedow described the agony of an Australian aboriginal he watched being cursed by a bone. The man stared with fear, his cheeks lost their colour and his whole face became distorted. His body started to shake and he died. On another similar occasion, a more powerful magician was able to lift the curse, after which the subject made a full and immediate recovery.

The Curse of Ho-tei

IN 1928, a middle-aged English couple, the Lamberts, purchased an ivory statue of the Japanese God of Good Luck, Ho-tei, from a shop in Kobe, Japan. The Lamberts were on a cruise, and when they returned to their ship, Marie Lambert stowed the statuette in her luggage en route to Manila. Two days later, she began to suffer from an excruciating toothache. She was prescribed painkillers, but they did little good. Mr and Mrs Lambert then came down with an unpleasant fever, with severe aching in the joints. Finally she managed to get to a dentist, but during treatment the drill slipped and drove through the nerve of her tooth, causing terrible pain.

THE STATUE'S CURSE

Ivory, which was used to carve the statue of Ho-tei that put a curse on whoever's possession it was in.

THE LAMBERTS next went to Australia, and the figurine was transferred to Mr Lambert's luggage. The following day, he too experienced an agonising toothache. He visited several dentists and even had a tooth extracted, but whenever he was in the cabin, the pain started again. The Lamberts finally worked out what was happening when they offered the gift to Mr Lambert's mother in the US. She was delighted, but when her teeth started to ache a few hours later, she handed back the gift claming that it was 'bad medicine'.

A GOD OF LUCK?

ONCE BACK in the UK, Mr Lambert took the statue to a Japanese art shop, where the manager offered to buy it. He explained that the Ho-tei was a temple god, and in the East, statues of such gods are sometimes given 'souls' in the form of small medallions hidden inside them. He arranged for an old man in Japanese national costume to place the statue in a shrine, and light incense. This appeared to appease the statue and Lambert assumed that the god of luck had been taking revenge on disbelievers who had removed him from his temple. Other experts suggested that the painful removal of the tusk from the elephant may have induced a form of psychic disturbance that manifested itself as severe toothache.

A Japanese carved ivory statue; these are sometimes believed to have souls.

King Tutankhamen

THE VALLEY of the Kings is one of the world's most impressive burial grounds and lies in a desert valley in Egypt, near the modern city of Luxor. For 500 years, the valley was a royal cemetery, where some of the most famous pharaohs of ancient Egypt were buried, surrounded by treasures, in tombs cut out of the valley cliffs.

Sponsored by a wealthy British aristocrat, Lord Carnarvon, a young archaeologist, Howard Carter, set out on a mission that would change our knowledge of Egyptian history. Since his first

visit to Egypt at the age of 16, Carter had always believed that there was at least one tomb still hidden in the Valley of the Kings, an area that had been exhausted by excavations and grave-robbers for many years.

The magnificent death mask of the pharaoh Tutankhamen, discovered when the tomb was opened in 1923.

THE TREASURE-HOUSE OF TUTANKHAMEN

AFTER SEVERAL DIGS over a number of years, Carter's team finally found some fragments bearing the name of Tutankhamen. The pieces led them to a gold-laden, treasure-filled room housing the tomb of King Tutankhamen. A party of 20 stood witness as Carter made his way into the room on 17 February 1923. Lord Carnarvon, however, did not live long to see the exquisite treasures. He died in April in the Hotel Continental in Cairo, after suddenly contracting an undiagnosed fever that racked his body for 12 days. Within minutes of his death there was a power failure in Cairo. At home in London, Carnarvon's dog died the same day. Interestingly, two weeks before his death, the writer Marie Corelli had warned that punishment would descend on anyone who violated Tutankhamen's tomb.

Lord Carnarvon, who died from a fever shortly after the tomb was excavated.

Howard Carter supervising the removal of treasures from the cursed tomb of King Tutankhamen.

THE PHARAOH'S WRATH

BEFORE THE YEAR was out, 12 of the original 20-strong
team were dead, and the deaths continued. George Jay Gould,
son of financier Jay Gould and a friend of Carnarvon's, came to
Egypt after his friend's death to see the site and he died of
bubonic plague within 24 hours of visiting the tomb. By 1929,
16 others who had come into contact with the mummy had
also died. Victims included radiologist Archibald Reid, who
had prepared the remains for X-rays, Lord Carnarvon's wife,
and Richard Bethell, his personal secretary. Even Bethell's
father committed suicide within the year.

WORDS OF WARNING

WAS THERE A CURSE on the tomb that had prevented it
being robbed across the centuries? Some people think so.
Although the tens of thousands of visitors to the site, and to
Tutankhamen's tomb,
which was the focus
of a worldwide
exhibition, have not
been affected by the
curse, there may be a
reason why only the
original party were
damned. The
hieroglyphics written
on the seal of the
entrance read: 'Death
will come on swift wings
to he who violates the
tomb of the Pharaoh.'

*Carter photographed at work on the
innermost coffin found in the tomb – the
one that contained the preserved body of
the pharaoh.*

The Barbados Coffins

IN 1812, on the island of Barbados, a strange
sequence of events occurred within a sealed
tomb. The family tomb was opened to bury
Colonel Thomas Chase, an affluent English-
man. His wife and two daughters respectively
had been placed in the tomb with no mishaps.
When the tomb was opened for a fourth time,
however, the coffins were found to be in complete disarray, as though they had been tossed
in the air and allowed to fall to the ground.
Anxious family members assumed that the
tomb had been vandalised (although there was
no evidence of this), and the coffins were duly
rearranged and the tomb tightly sealed again.

PHANTOM VANDALS?

HOWEVER, WHENEVER the tomb was
opened over the following eight years, it was
found in disorder. Finally, in 1820, the
governor of Barbados ordered the tomb
unsealed. He found that an earlier seal, all
other marks in the mortar and the sand laid
on the ground of the crypt were undisturbed,
yet the coffins were again in wildly different
positions around the tomb. One of the coffins

*A plan showing how the Barbados coffins were
originally placed, and how they were found after the
mysterious disturbances in the sealed tomb.*

THE COFFI

appears to have been thrown against the wall with such force that a deep gash was left in the stone. Surviving family members removed all the coffins and buried them elsewhere, where they remained untouched.

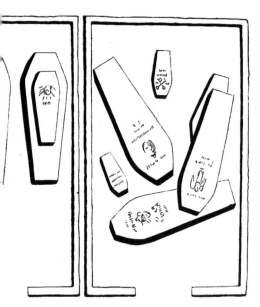

Y WERE PLACED.   THE COFFINS AS THEY WERE FOUND.

The doomed ship Scharnhorst.

The *Scharnhorst* Disaster

FEW SAILORS doubt that there are ships that have been jinxed, and one of the best-known examples is the German battleship *Scharnhorst*, which was launched in October 1936. When only half completed, the ship rolled on to its side, killing 60 workmen. Hitler and Goering arrived for the final launch to discover that the ship had somehow launched itself the previous night, destroying several barges.

THE JINX OF THE
SCHARNHORST

IN HER FIRST major engagement – the attack on the Danzig in 1939 – the *Scharnhorst*'s guns exploded, killing nine men, and the air supply system broke down, causing the deaths of 12 of the gunners. A year later, during the bombardment of Oslo, the ship was damaged and towed away. In the dark, she collided with the ocean liner *Bremen*, which settled into the river mud and was bombed by the British. After being repaired, the *Scharnhorst* was sent to

The ship's captain inspecting the crew before the Scharnhorst*'s fateful journey to the Arctic in 1943.*

the Arctic in 1943, but she was bombarded by several British cruisers. She was chased and finally hit, sinking to the bottom with most of her crew. Yet the curse apparently continued. Weeks later, two survivors from the damned ship were found washed up on the shore of a beach. They were both dead, having been killed by an emergency oil heater that had exploded when they tried to light it for warmth.

In his book on sea mysteries, *Invisible Horizons*, Vincent Gaddis writes, 'There are happy, gay ships, and there are others so impregnated with evil that they must be destroyed by fire'. Eventually, the *Scharnhorst* was brought to the surface and burned.

Graveyard Ships

THE *HINEMOA*

THE *HINEMOA* was a British vessel, launched in 1892. The sailors on board the ship knew that the ballast had been taken from a graveyard, and were wary of sailing her. During the voyage, four sailors died of typhoid. The ship's first captain went insane and the second ended up in prison. The third died of alcoholism, the fourth in mysterious circumstances in his cabin and the fifth committed suicide. The reason? The crew were unanimous: the combination of the graveyard ballast, and the bones of the four dead crew members, had jinxed the ship.

The unlucky ship Great Eastern, *which suffered a spate of disasters believed to be caused by a curse.*

THE *GREAT EASTERN*

THE *GREAT EASTERN* was another much-maligned and unlucky ship. As they did in the case of the *Hinemoa*, the crewmen believed that the bones of dead men were at the root of the ship's disasters. The ship was built by the famous Victorian engineer Brunel. He collapsed with a heart attack on her deck, and died soon after.

A riveter and his boy assistant vanished without trace during the ship's construction, and on its maiden voyage, a steam escape valve was left closed, causing an explosion that scalded five men to death. Its subsequent misfortunes were legendary – including explosions, collisions, accidents at sea and a spate of deaths among the crewmen. Finally, after 15 years, she was brought back to Milford Haven in South Wales, where she rusted and blocked the shipping lane. Breaking her up proved almost impossible and the wrecker's iron ball was invented in order to do so. Inside the double hull, the demolition experts discovered the skeletons of the riveter and his boy. Seamen believed the cause of the curse had been found.

The engineer Isambard Kingdom Brunel, who died soon after completion of the Great Eastern.

Famous Curses

THE BELL WITCH

JOHN AND LUCY BELL lived with their children on a farm
in Tennessee, USA. In 1817, one of the children, Elizabeth,
became the focus of malicious activity. In the beginning,

scraping sounds and other noises occurred, but soon her bedclothes and furniture were thrown around the room. She was subjected to horrendous physical attacks, which included being pinched, slapped, bruised and stuck with pins. The family believed she was being taunted by a spirit, which was 'nothing more nor less than old Kate Batts' witch'. Kate Batts was a local woman married to an invalid. She had once fallen out with Bell and had threatened to get even. She was still alive. John Bell eventually died a terrible death by poison, and the poltergeist continued to wreak havoc for seven years. The cause? No one in the area was in doubt – the Bell family had been cursed by Kate Batts, who was widely believed to be a witch.

THE CURSE OF PRINCESS AMEN-RA

IN 1868, the story of the mummy of an ancient Egyptian princess became headline news. Four young Englishmen bought the mummy of the princess. Soon after, one of them walked into the desert and vanished. Another of the buyers had his arm shot off, while a third had his bank fail and the last one became insolvent. The next owner of the mummy had three of his family injured in an accident and his house caught fire. The mummy was then given to the British Museum, where things continued to go wrong. Among an alleged catalogue of horrors were the deaths of porters and exhibits that were thrown about at night. The British Museum offered to sell the mummy to anyone who would buy it. According to legend, she was placed on the *Titanic* in 1912. Perhaps the mummy's curse caused the ship to strike an iceberg on her maiden voyage?

The witch that cursed the Bell family was believed to be Kate Batts, who sent a poltergeist to make physical attacks on the Bells.

MEDICAL CURIOSITIES

Introduction

OUR UNDERSTANDING of the human mind and body has developed dramatically over the past century, but there still remain many areas that defy explanation. For example, many parapsychologists confirm that the phenomena of ESP (extra-sensory perception), reincarnation, prophecy and premonition exist, despite scientific assertions to the contrary. What is the reason for their wholesale belief? Societies studying the paranormal around the world have documented and evidenced literally thousands of cases. Many medical curiosities elude scientific explanation as well. How can a woman glow in the dark, or a man become immune to electricity? How can a perfectly healthy teenager spontaneously burst into flames and burn to death within a matter of moments?

A young clairvoyant who can apparently see words hidden inside a sealed box.

THE SCIENCE OF THE PARANORMAL

IT IS TRUE that even medical literature is full of strange, grotesque and bizarre stories that cannot be explained. Some weight has to be given to the science of the paranormal, which seeks to explain what modern medicine and science dismiss. The paranormal is a vast area of human knowledge ranging from things that lie on the borderline of modern science to phenomena that most scientists would term nonsense. For each amazing discovery that is made, many new questions appear to challenge our intellect. The fact remains that many strange cases continue to occur around the world and, seemingly, after our life on Earth. Is it time we began to accept that there is more to the human body and spirit than science can prove?

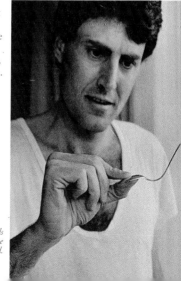

Uri Geller, who bends spoons using only the power of the mind.

The Luminous Woman

IN APRIL 1934, a young woman from the village of Pirano, Italy, developed a strange affliction that to this day has never been explained. Anna Manaro had just completed a religious fast when the condition began and some believed that the phenomena may have been a religious miracle. When Anna fell into a deep sleep, her body began to glow a vivid electric-blue colour in the chest area. The glow appeared to shine through the skin, and remained present until she awoke, when it suddenly disappeared.

On 11 April, Dr Protti from Padua University and a team of five other specialists undertook to investigate the cause of the disturbance, which had naturally excited much interest. They sat by her bedside at night and witnessed the phenomenon first-hand. During this time they took a variety of measurements and recorded the event on cine film.

Their research showed that during the period of 'glowing', Anna's heartbeat and respiratory rate doubled. Various theories were put forward, including the idea that Anna's blood had somehow become irradiated, but blood tests showed nothing untoward and this theory was abandoned. Anna was completely well apart from the strange glow and throughout the time it occurred showed no ill-effects whatsoever. The condition stopped, just as mysteriously as it had started, some three weeks later. She suffered no after-effects and the condition never recurred.

SHOCKPROOF ELECTRICIAN

The results of a study on an 80-year-old Bulgarian electrician called Ivanov were published in the *Bulgarian Medical Journal* in 1984. He appeared to have a natural immunity to electricity and never switched off the mains when undertaking domestic repairs. He had never had a shock, only a tingling sensation. Dr Georgi Tomasov took Ivanov to a Sofia hospital where specialists ran a series of tests. They found that his body appeared to be eight times as resistant to electricity as that of a normal person. No explanation was found.

Spontaneous Human Combustion (SHC)

THE EXTRAORDINARY phenomenon of spontaneous human combustion (SHC) has been recorded on some occasions, and has never been satisfactorily explained. It appears to occur when solitary humans have, in some unknown manner, burned up almost entirely, usually in a closed room, without setting fire to their surroundings beyond perhaps a hole in the floor, a chair and some nearby furnishings. Some believe that, as many of the subjects are elderly smokers, often alcoholic and known to take sleeping pills, this combination could lead to a person

The foot of John Irving Bentley – all that remained of him after his death by spontaneous human combustion.

catching fire. Interestingly, however, the flames seem to start from inside the person and younger people have also been affected. Whatever the cause, SHC is on the increase. No one knows why.

THE CINDER WOMAN

MARY REESER, a 67-year-old woman from St Petersburg, Florida, is now known as the 'cinder woman'. Sometime during the night of 2 July 1951, Mary went from being a completely healthy woman to nothing but a charred foot in a heap of ash the following morning. Nothing around her had been burned, and the plastic tiles that lay beneath her had not melted. Forensic scientists and fire-fighters were completely baffled. The FBI became involved, because of the suspicion of foul play, but this was soon ruled out. She died within three hours, which put paid to the idea that SHC victims burn slowly over the course of many hours, as previous evidence had suggested.

Mary Reeser, whose death baffled scientists and fire-fighters.

An incident of SHC was reported in a London nightclub, when a girl inexplicably burst into flames while dancing with her boyfriend.

LONDON NIGHTCLUB

A SIMILAR case occurred in a London nightclub when a girl, dancing with her boyfriend, suddenly erupted into flames and died on her way to the hospital. There were no other flames in the room. Her boyfriend declared that the flames had burst from her back, chest and shoulders, setting her hair alight.

HENRY THOMAS

IN JANUARY 1980, the remains of a 73-year-old Welshman, Henry Thomas from Ebbw Vale, were found by his sons-in-law in his home. He had been reduced to ashes, apart from his skull and still-trousered legs below the knee. An orange-red glow had been seen in the room. The window and lightbulb were covered in an orange substance. The television was still on, although its plastic knobs had melted. Yet a settee, only 1 m (3 ft) from the armchair in which Mr Thomas had been sitting, was unscathed.

THE CANDLE EFFECT

ONE POSSIBLE explanation of SHC has become known as the Candle Effect. This describes how, if a body is ignited and the fire is not put out, a gradual combustion process will take place in which the bones (like a candle wick) will be reduced to ash and the flesh (like the wax) will melt away. This explains why in most cases of SHC, little or no damage is found to the surroundings. Other research has suggested that the phenomenon may be caused by a combination of products in our diet causing a chemical chain reaction resulting in internal ignition; electricity and nuclear energy within the body have also been cited as other rational explanations.

A CURSED YEAR?
One of the strangest fact about spontaneous human combustion is that, although a reasonably rare occurence, 10 per cent of all known cases of the phenomomenon took place in the year 1980.

Psychic Surgery

ACCORDING TO the *Skepics' Dictionary,* 'Psychic "surgery" is a type of non-surgery performed by a non-medical healer. The healer fakes an incision by running a finger along a patient's body, apparently going through the skin without using any surgical instruments. The healer pretends to dig his hands into the patient's body and pretends to pull out "tumours". Using trickery, the healer squirts animal blood from a hand-held balloon while discarding items such as chicken livers and hearts. The patient then goes home to die, if he or she was really dying, or to live as if there was nothing seriously wrong in the first place'.

Can this phenomenon be dismissed so easily, though? According to some experts, psychic surgery is not just 'big business' – it represents an inexplicable, and in many cases successful, treatment of medical conditions requiring surgery or medication, without any physical trauma to the body.

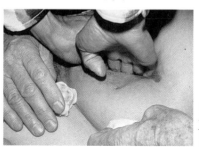

Feliciano Omilles, a psychic surgeon from the Philippines, at work in Mexico.

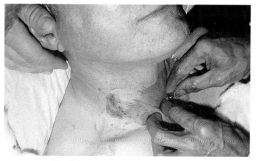

Many researchers believe that around 80 per cent of those practising psychic surgery are frauds – but there are those who seem to be genuine.

SLEIGHT-OF-HAND?

SOME RESEARCHERS believe that up to 80 per cent of those practising psychic surgery are fraudulent. The Philippines, where this form of healing began in the 1920s, is especially corrupt. So when a genuine psychic surgeon emerges, it is seen as an important discovery. South America, and in particular Brazil, came to prominence in this area in the 1960s, when one renowned healer, called Origo, became internationally known. Many of these healers 'channel' doctors. For example, Origo, who was nicknamed 'The Surgeon of the Rusty Knife', channelled a Doctor Fritz. Origo carried out a host of surgical procedures using nothing more than a rusty penknife. He was jailed twice for practising medicine illegally, but when a team of American doctors investigated him in 1968, they concluded that he was genuinely able to control an unknown form of life energy.

STEPHEN TUROFF

TODAY, THE UK is host to many widely respected healers, including Stephen Turoff. Turoff currently sees up to 50 people a day, five days a week, 52 weeks of the year. He has never had to advertise; his business comes through word of mouth.

According to the natural healing website (natural-healing.co.uk), Turoff is remarkable: 'When Turoff works, beautiful pastel lights descend like lightning bolts from the sky into patients' bodies, sacred ash forms on objects and people in his surgery, towels and sheets turn pink, and messages, finger-written in orange ochre, appear on photographs of saints. But most importantly, in many, many cases, the blind regain sight, the deaf hear, the lame cast away their crutches, diseased organs literally disappear and the sick and suffering are granted relief.'

Although this might sound like spiritual mumbo-jumbo, there are many people who believe that Turoff can, and does, work miracles.

HOW DOES IT WORK?

ACCORDING TO medical experts, the people who most often respond to psychic healing are those suffering from psychosomatic illnesses – disorders that are caused or aggravated by prolonged stress. This does not mean that the patient's problem is purely psychological. On the contrary, psychosomatic disorders can produce physical symptoms like acne, eczema, arthritis, headache, backache, asthma, sinusitis, hypertension, angina, constipation, impotence and infertility among others. In chronic pain disorders, for instance, the person has episodes of chronic pain that may last for months, yet no underlying cause is found. As with other psychosomatic ailments, these symptoms are the result of stress and the patient's way of getting the sympathy of others. As soon as the stress is gone – as soon as the person's anxiety is relieved – these symptoms disappear.

The respected Italian healer Nicola Cutolo undergoing tests in Germany to find out how his powers work.

ESP and Prophecy

EXTRA-SENSORY PERCEPTION (ESP) means the perception of objects, thoughts, or events without the use of the known human senses. Such perceptions, collectively called psi phenomena, are grouped in four main categories: telepathy, or mind-to-mind communication; clairvoyance, or the awareness of remote objects, persons, or events; precognition, or the knowledge of events lying in the future; and retrocognition, or the knowledge of past events in the absence of access to information about those events. Other forms of ESP include psychokinesis, the power to bend or shape objects through the influence of the mind.

Scientists have argued against paranormal researchers for decades about the possibility of ESP, and many tests have failed to prove that it exists. However, the files of the Society for Psychical Research in London are full of uncanny cases and the police have been known to use psychics in some of their investigations.

A computerised test for ESP in which a subject tries to pick which card the random process has chosen.

An experiment to assess the telepathic abilities of twins.

TAKE MY RING

On 9 September 1848, on the field of battle, a soldier was severely wounded and thought to be dying. He requested that his ring be removed and sent to his wife. His wife, who lay sleeping some 240 km (150 miles) away, woke up and had a vision of her husband being carried off the field. She heard his voice saying, 'Take this ring off my finger and send it to my wife.' The ring and the news of his death reached her several days later.

Uri Geller's Cadillac, covered in 5,000 pieces of bent cutlery, the phenomenon for which he has become famous.

BENDING SPOONS

URI GELLER became famous in the 1970s for his ability to bend metal by concentrating on it. Spoons, forks and keys allegedly continued to bend after he had left the room. Geller first became aware of these powers of psychokinesis (known as PK) when he was just four years of age. On countless occasions he has been able to read material in sealed envelopes, and to 'see' while blindfolded. His skills have been dismissed as trickery by some, but no one has been able to provide a rational explanation.

THE CINCINNATI PREMONITION

ONE OF the best documented cases of premonition occurred in 1979 in Cincinnati, Ohio. An office manager named David Booth had a vivid dream for 10 nights running, in which he 'saw' an American Airlines jet crashing into flames in an area full of buildings. Booth recognised that he was having a premonition, and contacted American Airlines, a psychiatrist and the Federal Aviation Authority. Finally, he was taken seriously and the FAA tried to link his dream with a particular type of aircraft. Then, on

26 May, a day after the last vision, an American Airlines DC10 took off from Chicago's O'Hare Airport. Seconds after it cleared the runway, an engine fell off and the plane crashed in a massive fireball at the edge of the airport and near to buildings on the site. Everyone on board was killed instantly.

After the accident, the Civil Aviation Authority confirmed that many details of the crash had matched Booth's dreams. Booth never understood why he was given advance notice of this event when he, and everyone else, was powerless to change it.

The Chicago air crash, which David Booth had premonitions of; despite his warnings to the authorities, they were powerless to prevent the disaster happening.

NOSTRADAMUS

MICHEL NOSTRADAMUS (Michel de Nostredame, 1503–66) was a French physician and astrologer, whose predictions of the future have fascinated people for centuries. Nostradamus acquired a great reputation as a doctor by treating victims of the plague that ravaged that part of Europe, but he eventually turned his interests to astrology and metaphysics. In 1555 he completed the *Centuries*, a book of more than 900 predictions about the fate of France, the world and celebrated persons of his time. The title of the book refers to the fact that the contents are arranged in sections of 100 verses each. An expanded version was published in 1558.

Some interpreters say the verses can be applied to anything, or nothing, whereas others claim that various verses foretold the Great Fire of London in 1666, the deaths of several monarchs, details of the French Revolution, the rise of both Napoleon and Hitler, and the Second World War.

Nostradamus, the French astrologer, whose predictions have fascinated the world since the sixteenth century.

VISIONS OF ABERFAN

ON 21 OCTOBER 1966, a huge spoil heap of coal slurry collapsed and buried a school in the mining town of Aberfan, South Wales. More than 140 people, including 128 school-children, were killed. During the weeks that followed, it became clear that many people had foreseen the tragedy. Thirty-five cases were recorded by British psychiatrist J. C. Barker.

One of the children killed in the slide had told her mother that she had had an odd dream: 'I dreamt I went to school,' she had explained, 'and there was no school there. Something black had come down all over it.' Two hours later she was dead in the tragedy. Her mother was comforted by the fact that the day before the disaster, her daughter had suddenly started talking about death, and explained that she wasn't afraid to die.

The Aberfan disaster, in which a spoil heap collapsed on a school; afterwards many predictions of the impending disaster were discovered.

Levitation

STRICTLY SPEAKING, levitation is the rising of a human body off the ground, in apparent defiance of the law of gravity. The term designates such occurrences in the lives of saints and of spiritualist mediums, generally during a seance; levitation of furniture and other objects during a seance has also been reported. Levitation of witches and other figures of folklore is called transvection and is said to involve the rubbing of 'flying ointment' on their bodies before flying to the Sabbat. The levitation of saints is usually directly upwards, whereas that of witches has the dynamic purpose of trans-portation. Theologians long debated whether transvection was illusion or fact; levitation, however, has been subject to less controversy, and there are many documented cases that appear to defy all reason.

Levitation is the rising of a body or object from the ground in defiance of gravity.

PSYCHOKINESIS

IN PARAPSYCHOLOGY, levitation is considered to be a phenomenon of psychokinesis, or 'mind over matter'. Most levitations last only a few seconds or perhaps a few minutes. Levitations of a spiritual nature are numerous in religion. Saints and mystics reportedly levitate as proof of the powers of God. For example, the seventeenth-century Christian saint

Joseph of Cupertino could allegedly levitate and fly about in the air for long periods of time. In Eastern mysticism, levitation is a feat made possible by the mastery of concentration and breathing techniques that control the universal life energy.

Many levitations have plausible natural explanations. A small minority do not, and have never been proved fraudulent.

The levitation of St Joseph of Cupertino.

DANIEL DUNGLAS HOME

THE SCOTTISH medium Daniel Dunglas Home (1833–86) was renowned for his remarkable physical feats, repeatedly moving objects, levitating, and materialising spirits. He was often accused of fraud, although no one was ever able to prove it. In the 1850s, when spiritualism came into vogue, he reportedly caused furniture and objects to rise and levitated himself on more than 100 occasions before witnesses. In 1868, he apparently floated in and out of windows. Unlike many mediums, he was not always in a trance during levitations and was aware of what was happening. He later said that an unseen power lifted him and he had 'an electrical fullness' in his feet.

Sceptics claimed that he hypnotised his audience into believing he was levitating, when in reality he was in his chair. However, many witnesses claim that this was not the case. One of the leading scientist of the day, Sir William Crookes, investigated Home's powers and stated that he could find no trace of deception.

Daniel Dunglas Home levitating.

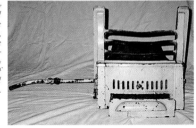

A gas fire from the Enfield poltergeist haunting, showing a bent pipe after inexplicably coming out of its normal position.

THE ENFIELD POLTERGEIST

IN LATE AUGUST 1977, the Harper family of Enfield, UK, was visited by a poltergeist which caused considerable disruption to the family's home. The events continued for some time and after the police, the local medium and a vicar were unable to help, the Harpers turned to the *Daily Mirror*, who were witness to many of the events. They had photographs of many alarming scenes, including one of the Harper children, Janet, floating in mid-air while asleep. Many objects were levitated with no apparent explanation, and none of the experts called in could find any evidence of trickery.

DEMONIC POSSESSION?

In 1906, a 16-year-old South African girl began to levitate uncontrollably, to a height of 1.5 m (about 5 ft). The only way that she could be brought down was to sprinkle her with holy water, suggesting that demonic possession was responsible.

Reincarnation and
Past Lives

REINCARNATION INVOLVES the idea that the spirit of a person leaves the body at death and is reborn into someone else. In Hinduism and Buddhism, it is believed that the spirit passes either to a higher or lower form of life, depending on the righteousness of the life just left, while Christians believe that Jesus was reincarnated after he died on the cross. Is reincarnation just a religious belief or actual fact?

MARY SUTTON

IN 1993 A WOMAN from Northamptonshire, Jenny Cockell, claimed that from an early age she was beset by dreams of a woman in a cottage, with a large family and an abusive husband. Jenny was haunted by these dreams, despite growing up and having her own family. She was convinced that the woman lived in Ireland, and was able to draw maps of the town and the household from memory. Feeling that unfinished business was the

Jenny Cockell, who believes she lived a past life in Ireland.

cause of the dreams, she travelled to Ireland and located the village. She discovered that the long-dead woman of her dreams had lived in a cottage outside Dublin. She'd been named Mary Sutton and after her death at an early age, her children had been separated and sent off to foster homes. They'd never seen one another again. Jenny decided that it was her responsibility to resolve this and tracked down several of the surviving children. She organised a reunion in the house they had all shared. The children were astonished by the intimate details of their childhood that this woman could provide, particularly since Jenny was years younger than Mary Sutton. Was this reincarnation? Or was Jenny Cockell haunted by an unhappy ghost?

Each Dalai Lama is believed to be a reincarnation of his predecessor.

THE DALAI LAMA

Dalai Lama is the title of the religious leader of Tibetan Buddhism, who was also, until 1959, temporal ruler of Tibet. Each Dalai Lama is believed to be the reincarnation of his predecessor. When one dies, the new incarnation is sought among newly born boys; the child is identified by his ability to pick out possessions of the former Dalai Lama from a group of similar objects.

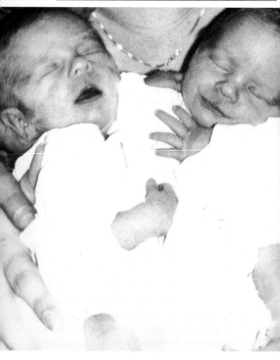

Some evidence suggests that the Pollock twins might be reincarnations of their older sisters who had been killed in a road accident.

THE POLLOCK TWINS

IN 1957, two sisters aged 6 and 11, and the only children of the Pollock family from Hexham in Northumberland, were tragically run over. Along with a male schoolmate, they were killed outright by a woman who had decided to take her own life.

Their father, John Pollock, was a strong believer in reincarnation and when his wife announced she was pregnant some months later, he prophesied that she would bear twin girls who would be their daughters reincarnated.

PROOF OF REINCARNATION

THE FAMILY DOCTOR detected only one foetus in the womb and Florence Pollock refused to believe her husband. However, on 4 October 1958, twin girls were delivered. One of the twins had a faint white mark on her forehead that matched a scar on the head of one of the dead daughters. The other twin had an identical birthmark to the other dead daughter. The strange coincidences did not stop there. The children recognised the school that their sisters had attended, knew uncanny facts about the dead girls' childhoods, and could correctly name their older siblings' dolls (and knew which one had belonged to each). More frightening still, they were often found together, one cradling the other, and talking about blood pouring from her mouth, just as it had during the accident. Once, when a car started up that was facing them at the same angle as the car which killed their older sisters, they screamed and clutched each other in terror.

The incidents ceased when the twins reached five years of age, and they had no recollection of them. The case has never been satisfactorily explained.

Miracles

Introduction

No OTHER FORM of apparition or vision has such an emotionally overwhelming effect as the sighting of the Virgin Mary, the mother of Jesus. Some of these visions are accompanied by other events, such as weeping, bleeding or even moving statues.

RELIGIOUS VISIONS

VISIONS OF the Virgin Mary are widely attested to by individuals and whole communities around the world. While one or only a small group of people may witness the actual vision, pilgrims and other witnesses experience all types of paranormal phenomena, such as burning bushes, heavenly music and

Ivy Wilson took this picture of a rainbow, but when the photograph was developed, an image of the Virgin Mary and Jesus appeared on the print.

A vision of the Virgin Mary seen by an art restorer in a church in Hungary.

visions of a spinning sun. The tears of a weeping statue, the waters from a holy spring, or the directed spiritual energy of a healer have been known to produce miracles. People's lives have been saved and dramatically changed by contact with these phenomena. But how much of this really lies in the power of the mind?

COLLECTIVE VISIONS

SOME THEORISTS ALLEGE that it is the power of collective faith that triggers these miracles. Others believe that people see what they want to see, and that their intense concentration is responsible for physical changes, both in their bodies and to their environment. But what of the fact that many witnesses are children, or unwilling and unwitting visionaries? How can we explain what happened at Fatima (see page 134), where tens of thousands of people saw something miraculous happen?

Miracles happen both to those who believe and those who do not. They illustrate another part of the human body and mind, and the world around us, that we may never be able to understand.

The Madonna of Medjugorje

LATE IN the afternoon of 24 June 1981, six children – four girls and two boys, some together and some alone – witnessed a vision of the Virgin Mary on a rural hillside. She told the children she would return the next day, and every day thereafter.

This amazing story took place in the tiny village of Medjugorje, in Bosnia-Herzegovina. Medjugorje is now a major centre of pilgrimage, attracting millions of visitors from around the world. Within three days of the first encounter, 15,000 people congregated on the hill to see the Virgin. A bright light shone over the village before the apparition, and the word 'Mir' or 'Peace' was once emblazoned in the sky in red. Strange lights regularly played across the giant cross that was erected on the next hill in 1983.

WHAT HAPPENED?

FOR MORE THAN five years, the visions occurred, although only the original six children could see the Virgin herself. The children appeared to go into a kind of trance during visits, and medical checks showed them to be immune to stimuli and even pain during these periods. The trances seemed genuine and the children returned with detailed messages and prophecies. By 1985, the children had had more than 2,000 visions between them, and the Virgin told them it would be her last appearance on Earth.

Scientists have not been able to find an explanation for this manifestation of the Madonna. Even the most advanced research techniques of psychologists and neurologists have proved inadequate to throw light on the phenomenon.

A Dutch professor of theological psychology, Dr J. Weima, concluded, after submitting the group to regular and thorough physical and psychological examinations, that there is no question of deceit or derangement. Dr Weima affirms that something very unusual is being perceived which others cannot see, but as to exactly what happens, he concludes: 'Science, as it is at present, has not yet found an explanation.'

An illustration showing the Blessed Virgin appearing to the children in the village of Medjugorje.

The Fatima Miracle

O**N 13 MAY 1917**, two nine-year-olds and a seven-year-old saw a 'brilliant lady in white' while working in a field in the rural area of Fatima in Portugal. The woman was described as being radiant, and she appeared from a beam of light that flashed from the sky. She said that she had come from heaven and asked the children to return on the 13th day of each month.

THE ANGEL IN THE SKY

THE LOCAL RESIDENTS were astonished by the suggestion that an angel had appeared to the three children, and word soon spread. On the 13th of each month a crowd gathered to watch and although only the original three witnesses ever saw the 'angel' again, many believed that they had been visited by the Virgin Mary. More than 20,000 people had turned up to witness the miracle by September. According to witnesses

a 'luminous globe' travelled across the sky from east to west. On 13 October, the children saw a vision at noon precisely, and some 70,000 came to watch. One of the girls announced that she had seen the Holy Family in the sky,

The three children who first saw the vision of a 'brilliant lady in white' at Fatima.

People flocked to Fatima after news of the miracle spread – here they witness the solar phenomenon.

and the crowd looked up to see the sun 'whirling and dancing in the sky'. Many onlookers claimed that a hole was punched through the rain cloud at noon, and a spinning disk (the Sun) poured down blinding radiance and great heat on the ground before swirling back up again. The visions stopped after October and never recurred.

No photographs of the miracle exist, but there were literally thousands of witnesses. Prophecies had also been given to the children, one for the imminent Russian Revolution, one for the Second World War and a third that was long held in the Vatican in a sealed envelope, the contents of which were revealed in 2000. One of the interpretations of this third vision was a prophecy of the attempted assassination of the pope in 1981.

Statues, Icons and Miracles

ACCORDING TO a 1998 BBC news report, thousands of visitors have flocked to see a 'bleeding Christ' statue in Calcutta. A lawyer who live in the compound of a church in the city said she saw blood coming from wounds of the Christ figure on a 45-cm (18-in) cross at her home. 'I went to clean it and noticed it was bleeding from where Christ was nailed and where the crown of thorns was,' said Ajanta Rovena Chatterjee. More than 10,000 people have since prayed at the icon.

SOUTH AMERICAN MIRACLE

IN THE working-class La Cisterna district in the south of Santiago, Chile, a small blue-and-white porcelain statue belonging to Olga Rodriguez, a housewife, began to weep blood in November 1992. Doctors attached to the police Criminal Investigation Department confirmed that the mysterious red liquid which flowed from the eyes of the statue of the Virgin Mary was human blood. Dr Inelia Chacon, working on the project, confirmed that three samples of the liquid

A statue of the Virgin Mary weeping tears of blood, 1982.

examined in a laboratory were shown to be blood. According to the *Guardian* newspaper: 'The Santiago coroner's office pronounced the substance is type O-4 human blood. The statue weeps regularly, particularly in the presence of children.'

A weeping statue of the Virgin Mary in Brooklyn, New York, 1984.

THE VIRGIN OF GUADELOUPE

IN THE GARDEN shrine of Pablo Covarrubias stands a statue of the Virgin of Guadeloupe, brought from the Basilica in Mexico City. Since 1998, the Virgin has regularly wept real tears that are then harvested in little cotton balls and distributed to the faithful. According to Pablo, many supernatural healings have been documented, and on one very windy day, an apparition of Mary appeared in the sky above the shrine.

THE WEEPING MADONNA

IN A BACK ROOM of the Post Office in the tiny southern Ireland village of Grangecon, County Wicklow, the post mistress Mary Murray keeps her statue of the Virgin Mary. The painted statue stands about 30 cm (12 in) high and is housed in a sealed glass case. BBC2's *Everyman* programme told, on 18 December 1994, how the statue had been found to be 'crying blood'. The statue, with its blood-stained cheeks, was clearly shown to viewers. At 3 p.m. every day, the glass case with its holy contents is taken, to the accompaniment of Hail Marys, to be placed beside the outdoor shrine of the Madonna nearby.

CHICAGO, 1997

HUNDREDS OF Christians regularly visit the home of Salim Najjar in North Hirschberg, Chicago, where an image of the Madonna has appeared in a window and a small picture of an icon produces tears. An Orthodox Christian bishop officially proclaimed these events to be 'an extension of the miracle of Our Lady of Cicero' – an icon at the St George Church in Cicero that began weeping.

Salim Najjar said that when the image of the Madonna appeared on his front window, the amazed family, who attend the St George Church, taped a small reproduction of the weeping icon to the window. To their astonishment the small picture began giving off oily tears.

The weeping Madonna in County Wicklow, Ireland.

THE CARDINAL AND THE VIRGIN MARY

BLURRED IMAGES on two photographs taken during the requiem mass for England's Cardinal Basil Hume could be the Virgin Mary, claimed one of the photographers. The two photographs were taken at exactly the same time during the service in September 1999. Terence Wynn, a photographer for the *Northern Cross* newspaper, took his photograph from the television. He said the same image appeared on another photograph taken at exactly the same time – and also from television – by a priest in Hartlepool. Mr Wynn believes the translucent image resembles the statue of the Immaculate Conception, Our Lady of Lourdes, which is in the grotto at Lourdes (see page 140).

A photograph of the funeral mass for Cardinal Basil Hume. Two other photographs taken at the same time show a blurred image of the Virgin Mary.

Lourdes and St Bernadette

IN 1858, in the grotto of Massabielle, near Lourdes in southern France, the Virgin Mary appeared 18 times to Bernadette Soubirous, a young peasant girl. Mary revealed herself as the 'Immaculate Conception'. Bernadette described her as 'a girl in white no bigger than myself'. The vision spoke to Bernadette and asked that a chapel be built at the site of the visitation. She also told the girl to drink from a fountain in the grotto. There was no fountain in evidence, and Bernadette scrabbled in the mud, to the amusement of onlookers, in an attempt to dig for a stream. The following day, there was a clear stream running where Bernadette had been digging, and the water from the stream immediately restored sight to a blind man.

An apparition of the Virgin Mary appears to St Bernadette at Lourdes in 1858.

LOURDES AND ST BERNADETTE

The water from this spring still flows and it has been shown to have a remarkable healing power, though it contains no curative property that science can identify. Lourdes has become the most famous modern shrine of the Virgin Mary.

Bernadette, after enduring a period of painful publicity, entered a convent at Nevers, France, where she remained until her death. She was canonised in 1933.

Pilgrims at the grotto in Lourdes where the vision appeared to Bernadette Soubirous.

THE MOST BLESSED VIRGIN

IN 1962, the results of a four-year enquiry by the Catholic Church into events at Lourdes were published. The Bishops' Commission concluded: 'We have also sought the opinion of scientists and we are finally convinced that the Appearance is supernatural and divine, and that consequently, She whom Bernadette has seen is the Most Blessed Virgin Herself. Our conviction is based, not merely upon the testimony of Bernadette herself, but more especially upon the events which have taken place and which can only be explained by divine intervention.'

Stigmata

STIGMATA ARE wounds on the body which bear a resemblance to the wounds of Christ when he was crucified on the cross. The people who suffer from stigmata are often nuns, priests or people with strong religious beliefs. Stigmata do not always appear in the same way. One stigmatic, for example, might only have the wounds that would have been made by the crown of thorns, while another might experience only a lance-wound in the side, or the wounds in the wrists or palms of the hands, or in the feet. The wounds from which stigmatics suffer are almost always identical to the wounds shown on the statues of Jesus to which they pray: if the statue has nails in the palms, blood will flow from the sufferer's palms.

VISIBLE AND INVISIBLE STIGMATA

PHYSICAL WOUNDS are called visible stigmata. Other ecstatics might only experience the suffering, without any outward marks – this phenomenon is known as invisible stigmata. Many experts consider stigmata

Stigmatics experience wounds in the hands, palms, feet or sides, that resemble the wounds sustained by Christ at the Crucifixion.

The Italian stigmatic Giorgio Bongiovanni, who received his stigmata during a visit to Fatima.

to be one of the most baffling and intriguing of medical and scientific mysteries. The most common theory about stigmata is that the sufferers have caused it themselves by the power of their own mind and the strength of their beliefs. Science has yet to explain the phenomenon. Religious theorists argue that this is the power of faith.

ST FRANCIS OF ASSISI

St Francis of Assisi (1186–1226) had stigmata of a character that has never been seen since. In the wounds of his feet and hands were excrescences of flesh representing nails – those on one side having round back heads, those on the other having rather long points, which bent back and grasped the skin. Many of his brethren were witness to the wounds, and a number of contemporary historians have confirmed their existence.

PADRE PIO

IN SEPTEMBER 1918, a 31-year-old Capuchin monk, Padre Pio, saw a mysterious person whose 'hands, feet and side were dripping blood'. He said: 'The sight terrified me and what I felt at that moment is indescribable. I thought I should die, and really would have died if the Lord had not intervened and strengthened my heart which was about to burst out of my chest. The vision disappeared and I became aware that my hands, feet and

Padre Pio showing his stigmata in the backs of his hands.

side were dripping blood. Imagine the agony I experienced and continued to experience almost every day. The heart wound bleeds continually, especially from Thursday evening until Saturday.'

Although he found the wounds 'embarrassing', and prayed for the visible marks to be removed, he did not ask for relief from the pain. He believed that the wounds, which stayed with him for 50 years, gave him the strength to fend off attacks by the devil.

PIO THE SAINT

MANY WERE suspicious of Padre Pio and his miraculous wounds. The Vatican even bugged the padre's confessional and opened his post. He was also banned from saying Mass for many years. But the present pope, who travelled from Poland to visit Padre Pio in 1947, accepted him back into the Church's fold and honoured him with the title 'The Venerable'. Beatification – an honour that usually leads to sainthood – requires evidence that the candidate has been responsible for working miracles. In 1991, a woman who had been hospitalised for a burst lymph vessel made a rapid recovery after praying for the padre's intervention. After investigating the case at length, the Vatican declared the cure to be authentic and 'extraordinary' – evidence enough to put Padre Pio on the path to sainthood.

Relics of Padre Pio, including a plastic box of dried blood which fell from his hands when he removed his mittens for Mass.

The Turin Shroud

THE SHROUD of Turin is a centuries-old linen cloth that bears the image of a crucified man – a man that millions believe to be Jesus of Nazareth. The shroud has been the object of much detailed study and intense research. Many experts have concluded that it was the cloth that wrapped the crucified body of Christ, although the controversy is still intense.

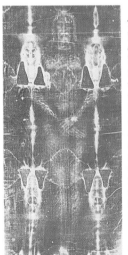

CHEMICAL TESTS

THE SHROUD, WIDELY believed to be Christ's burial cloth, bears a faded image of a bearded man and what appear to be bloodstains that coincide with Christ's crucifixion wounds. The 4-m (13-ft) long linen cloth has been kept in the city of Turin, Italy, since 1578. American biochemist Dr Alan Adler established in 1988 that the shroud image was indeed that of a person, and the blood came from violently inflicted wounds. He said blood flowing from wounds has a different chemistry to blood that flows

The Turin Shroud, widely believed to be the cloth in which Christ was buried.

in veins. But he said he couldn't prove whether the image on the shroud was Christ's. 'We know for sure it's human blood and it came from a man who died a traumatic death,' Adler said in a 1998 interview. 'There's no laboratory test for "Christ-ness".'

THE FORGERY CONTROVERSY

SOME EXPERTS suggest that the shroud is a medieval fake. However, its mystery continues to puzzle scientists. No one is sure how the startling image of Christ was produced, but an experiment in 1999 managed to create a replica of the shroud image by covering a human subject with aloe and myrrh.

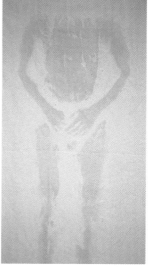

This is the result of the experiment to reproduce the shroud image using aloe and myrrh on a human subject.

To the believers, the cloth is a miracle and a sign of Christ's divinity that no amount of scientific tests could explain. One investigator suggested that it was created by 'a sudden radiance of Our Lord's body at the moment of resurrection'.

Spiritual Healing

SPIRITUAL HEALERS focus their attention on the highest source of peace and love in the universe that they can imagine, whatever their spiritual beliefs. This is called 'attunement to the universal source' and is similar to meditation. It is a state of heightened awareness: being totally present and at the same time having an attitude of detachment.

Spiritual healers consciously direct this experience of union with the universal source through themselves to the patient. This is called channelling. This type of healing, where a patient is present, is sometimes called 'laying on of hands', although the hands are mainly held a short distance from the body. At the end of a healing session, healers will consciously break the connection they have made with the patient and resume their normal everyday conscious state of being.

HEALING IN JAPAN

IN SEPTEMBER 1994, a Japanese experiment took place. Carol Everett, a healer from Devon in the UK, was flown to Tokyo's Denki University to participate in tests with Professor Yoshio Machi. She was hooked up to a series of monitors which would chart changes in her body and mind during the healing process. She was introduced to a girl she had never met before, and correctly diagnosed a lump on one of the woman's ovaries. Carol then began a healing process to remove the tumour, which was about 2 cm across. During the healing, changes were noted in the healer's brain activity, and at the same time, the image of the patient on the scanner altered radically. The heat intensity of the tumour cooled and the spot reduced until, after seven minutes, it disappeared completely. Carol came out of her trancelike state, and the imaging equipment confirmed that she was right. A month later, the girl's doctor confirmed that the tumour was completely gone.

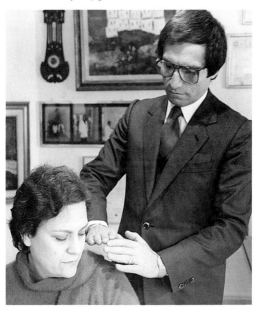

An Italian psychic performing a spiritual healing.

LITTLE PEOPLE

Introduction

FAIRIES ARE generally believed to be a type of supernatural being, neither ghost, god nor demi-god, which exists on Earth and either helps or harms humankind. Fairy beliefs are widespread and, across many cultures around the world, they are remarkably similar.

THE ORIGINS OF FAIRIES

THERE IS no absolute agreement on the origins of the many varieties of fairies. Some suggest that they are the dispossessed spirits of humans not yet ready for heaven. Others believe that they are a distinct life-form capable of multiplying by means of the usual reproductive process. In Devon, in the UK, one

Illustration showing 'the world of fairies' – are these just folklore, or do they really exist?

Fairies have fascinated us for centuries, although sightings of fairies are rare and largely unsubstantiated.

tradition is that they are the spirits of infants who died before baptism. Folklorists and anthropologists have theorised that the original fairies were members of conquered races who took to the hills and whose descendants were sighted on rare occasions.

SIMPLY FOLKLORE?

BESIDES THE speculations of scholars and folk explanations, all that is known with any certainty is that wherever they come from, fairy beliefs exist in every traditional society. And the fact remains that fairies are sighted and documented by reliable witnesses, even in the twentieth century. Are they an illusion? Like many aspects of the paranormal, fairy sightings remain on the fringes of human experience.

While there is no convincing proof that they exist, neither is there proof that they do not, and many acclaimed and respected individuals, such as Sir Arthur Conan Doyle, have been willing to swear to being witness to the phenomenon. Even if we do not understand the underlying basis – be it psychological or paranormal – the stories told of fairy sightings are marvellous, and there to be marvelled at.

The Cottingley Fairies

IN 1917, TWO Yorkshire children, Elsie Wright and Frances Griffiths, claimed that they had met and photographed fairies. The photographs were sent to Sir Arthur Conan Doyle, who was intrigued enough to send a friend to interview them. Upon examining the photographs, Conan Doyle published a book entitled *The Coming of the Fairies* (1922), in which he confirmed that he believed the photographs to be genuine. The photographs were taken to the Kodak laboratory in London, and Doyle later wrote: 'Two experts were unable to find any flaw, but refused to testify to the genuineness of them, in view of some possible trap.'

PHOTOGRAPHING FAIRIES

BOTH GIRLS CLAIMED that they had seen fairies several times behind their homes at Cottingley in Yorkshire and, unable to convince their parents of the fact, they had undertaken to capture them on film. The first photographs were taken in 1917; further photographs were taken in 1920.

The case of the Cottingley Fairies is one of the most famous sightings of the 'little people'.

One of the Cottingley fairy photographs: Frances Griffiths with a fairy, photographed by her friend Elsie Wright.

The *Strand* magazine published Doyle's first article with the original two pictures at Christmas the same year, and the following March a follow-up on the latter three. The story received worldwide publicity, and almost everyone considered the photographs to be fakes.

In August 1921, a noted psychic was sent to Cottingley and he saw the fairies along with Frances. No photographs could be taken that day, so apart from the word of the psychic and, once again, the girls, there was no further proof that the fairies existed.

For years afterwards attempts to debunk the photographs failed, and the two girls stood by their story. However, in 1972, Elsie sent the two cameras, along with other material related to the case, to Sotheby's for sale and with them a letter confessing for the first time that they had faked the photographs. Three years later, however, when interviewed by *Woman* magazine, Elsie and Frances gave the impression that the photographs were, after all, real.

Elsie Wright photographed with a fairy at Cottingley Glen in West Yorkshire.

A HOAX?

FINALLY, SHORTLY before Elsie and Frances died, both finally confessed that four photographs were outright hoaxes. They pointed to the fact that you could see the head of a hat pin that was holding up the gnome. It was sticking out of the figure's chest, although Conan Doyle had thought this to be a psychic umbilical cord. As for the fifth image, it was slightly less two-dimensional and clear. Elsie said that it was also a hoax, but until her death Frances was adamant that it was the only real fairy photograph they ever took.

HOW DID THEY DO IT?

IN 1982, an issue of the *Unexplained* and the *British Journal of Photography* reopened the case, and published extensive investigations by the *BJP*'s editor Geoffrey Crawley. It was revealed that the girls had agreed that the pictures were a practical joke to be continued until after the deaths of everyone involved. Elsie, a gifted artist, had apparently created the figures, using as her models fairies depicted in a popular children's book *Princess Mary's Gift Book*. Elsie and Frances complained that

the 'confessions' were unauthorised and untrue.

In the 1980s, Elsie finally showed how she and Frances had taken the fake photographs, using paper cut-out fairies. Despite this, both women – even on their death beds – insisted that regardless of the status of their photographs, there were real fairies and elves in Cottingley Beck and that they, and others, saw them.

Elsie Wright in the 1980s, with a paper cut-out of a fairy to show how she and Frances faked their fairy photographs.

Fairy Rings

ACCORDING TO FOLKLORE, fairies often dance in circles in the grass. These formations are known as fairy rings and they spell danger for human passers-by. The fairy music can be so enchanting that a person may be led into the ring where they remain captive forever in the fairy world. If a human steps into the ring they will become trapped in the wild dancing and may become lost to the sight of their companions who can hear the music but see nothing. The interlude might seem to last only two minutes, or at most a whole night, but outside of the ring years can elapse.

A man is pulled back before he enters a fairy circle, compelled to join the dancing.

NATURE'S CHARM

WE NOW KNOW, however, that the circles are formed by a collection of fungi growing in a ring formation. The fungus is known as the fairy ring champignon (*Marasmius oreades*). The young mycelia spread outward as the fungus gets older and its outer rim produces the fruiting bodies in a ring. Mycelia help the grass absorb nutrients and hence the grass becomes darker in the 'fairy ring'.

A 'fairy ring' made of fungi.

FAIRY VOICES?

In 1972, while strolling along the shore of a peninsula in the Scottish Highlands, American folk singer Artie Traum heard disembodied voices chanting 'Run, man, run' in a strange harmony to the sound of fiddles and pipes. When Traum fled to a nearby wood, he heard crackling sounds and 'great motion'. He later said, 'my head was swarming with thousands of voices, thousands of words making no sense'. The voices ceased when he found his way back to the open air.

Famous Sightings

FAIRY PLAYMATES

EDGAR CAYCE was one of the twentieth century's most famous psychics and he had an extraordinary ability to diagnose health problems by taking psychic readings. His psychic talents first manifested themselves in childhood, when he played in his garden with a host of 'imaginary friends'. These 'nature playmates', as his mother called them, were a secret between mother and son because of the ridicule he received at school when he described them. Many years later Cayce read about the fairy realm and realised that perhaps his playmates had been real.

BRIGHT LITTLE PEOPLE

ON 30 APRIL 1973, a London woman named Mary Treadgold was travelling by bus through the Scottish Highlands. The bus pulled over to let an oncoming car pass and Treadgold saw,

outside her window, a 'small figure, about 45 cm (18 in) high, a young man with his foot on a spade arrested in the act of digging.... He had a thin keen face (which I would know again, tight, brown, curly hair, was dressed in bright blue bib and braces, with a very white shirt with rolled-up sleeves. An open sack, also miniature,

The American psychic healer Edgar Cayce who had fairy playmates in his youth.

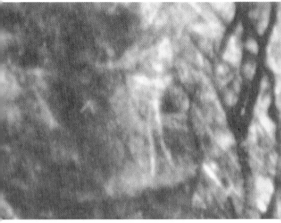

A photograph taken by John L. Hall who experienced strange and frightening sensations and heard music while visiting Glen Aldyn on the Isle of Man; afterwards he found a tiny person in the foliage.

stood at his side. He was emphatically not a dwarf nor a child, nor (last desperate suggestion of a sceptic) a plastic garden gnome. He was a perfectly formed living being like any of us, only in miniature.' Treadgold later mentioned the story to a Highland friend, and was told that the area was known for sightings of small people, who lived happily among them. The descriptions were of very 'bright' people. She later said, 'This ... I do recollect in the brightness of the hair and clothes, and the general appearance of energy and alertness'.

THE ANCIENT AND NATURAL WORLD

Introduction

FOR ALL THE ANSWERS that have been offered for the unexplained phenomena we have discussed so far, new mysteries still present themselves on a regular basis. In many ways, the most ancient of mysteries are those that continue to elude us, for all the many years if investigation and study that have gone into attempting to discover their meaning and purpose. We can analyse Stonehenge and other megaliths, but will we ever understand their real significance, or come to terms with how a body of primitive people were able to create such physically challenging monuments? What about the pyramids? How could such wonders have been created and, indeed, have survived to this day? Will we ever know how birds are more successful navigators than highly trained pilots with expensive and up-to-the-minute technology? What secrets lie deep in the earth – or high above it – and create mysteries such as crop circles? Could they be more than a hoax? Since the dawn of time, man has recognised the power of Nature and has sought to understand it.

The fact is that the universe is enigmatic, and in order to appreciate its depth and breadth, we need to open our minds to the idea that there may be forces afoot that cannot be explained in purely scientific terms.

The mysterious ancient site of Stonehenge on Salisbury Plain, Wiltshire.

Stonehenge

STONEHENGE IS THE MOST famous prehistoric megalithic monument in Europe. Excavations and radiocarbon dating have revealed that Stonehenge has an exceptionally long history of use as a ceremonial or religious centre. It was built in four distinct stages, from *c.* 2800 BC to *c.* 1100 BC.

Among the megalithic monuments of Europe, Stonehenge is unique because of its long period of use, the precision of its plan and its architectural details.

The precision of its plan and its architectural details make Stonehenge unique among ancient monuments.

STUDYING STONEHENGE

IN 1963, Gerald Hawkins, Professor of Astronomy at Boston University, USA, stated that Stonehenge was like a giant computer: a huge observatory capable of extremely complex calculations based on the position of the sun, moon and stars. When Hawkins fed all the data he had about the site into a computer, he found that the stones could be used to predict the occurrence of eclipses. His theory was corroborated by the work of C. A. Newman, who said that the highly educated astronomer priests of the time could have stood in the centre of the great circle and determined the position of the sun or moon in their orbits by using the stones as a guide.

Professor Sir Fred Hoyle, one of Britain's most famous astronomers, supported the theory that Stonehenge was a giant observatory. He agreed that the megaliths could be used as markers to gauge the moon's activity as it passed through different stages of its cycle. He noted

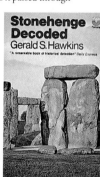

that Stonehenge's construction 'demanded a level of intellectual attainment higher than the standard to be expected from a community of primitive farmers'.

If these academics are right, Stonehenge and other standing-stone sites were designed for making complex astronomical observations at a time when there was no form of written word.

Gerald Hawkins' book Stonehenge Decoded, *in which he puts forward theories for the possible purpose of this mysterious site.*

Chico Stones

O N 8 MARCH 1922, stones varying in size from small pebbles to large rocks began cascading down on the roof of a grain warehouse and several surrounding houses near the railway tracks at Chico, California. The 'rain' lasted for seven days and despite a full-scale police operation on the site, no explanation was ever found. The local fire chief and police officer, who were investigating the riddle, had a narrow escape when a large boulder crashed out of the sky on to to a fence beside them, in front of several witnesses.

Charles Fort, a virtual hermit who investigated unexplained phenomena for decades in the US and UK, wrote several books, including *The Book of the Damned* (1919). He had an explanation for falling objects: he believed that these objects come from the Super-Sargasso Sea,

Caricature of Charles Fort, whose books offer explanations for falling objects.

which is a 'region somewhere above the Earth's surface in which gravitation is inoperative'. He believed that 'things raised from this Earth's surface to that region have been held there until shaken down by storms'. An imaginative concept, certainly, and one that garnered some following in its day.

The cover of Fate *magazine from May 1958, showing a shower of frogs.*

FROG FALLS

- Pliny records strange rain of frogs AD 77
- In Sutton Park, Birmingham, UK, hundreds of frogs peppered people's umbrellas during a summer shower in 1954.
- On a golf course in Arkansas, in 1973, players watched as thousands of frogs came down during a rainstorm.
- In 1977, at Canet-Plage in France, frogs the size of peas were seen bouncing off the bonnets of people's cars.
- In 1979, a housewife from Bedford, UK, found not only frogs all over her lawn following a rainstorm, but also frog spawn hanging from the bushes.

Bird Migration

IN AN AGE OF increasing technological knowledge, the navigational instincts of migrating birds still remain a mystery to mankind. Without the use of compasses or any type of electronic gadgetry, birds follow specific routes across the skies, sometimes in narrow, well-defined air tunnels, sometimes on broad fronts often hundreds of kilometres across. The physical effort, along with the navigational achievement, is extraordinary.

It has long been known that birds possess an uncanny compass sense and an innate ability to fly in a single constant direction, regardless of their point of departure. How is it done?

NAVIGATIONAL SENSORS

MANY BIRDS seem capable of sensing their location in relation to the sun, using this to navigate. Celestial navigation, using the stars, also appears quite common. On partially clouded nights their ability to navigate with only restricted

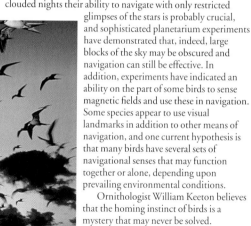

glimpses of the stars is probably crucial, and sophisticated planetarium experiments have demonstrated that, indeed, large blocks of the sky may be obscured and navigation can still be effective. In addition, experiments have indicated an ability on the part of some birds to sense magnetic fields and use these in navigation. Some species appear to use visual landmarks in addition to other means of navigation, and one current hypothesis is that many birds have several sets of navigational senses that may function together or alone, depending upon prevailing environmental conditions.

Ornithologist William Keeton believes that the homing instinct of birds is a mystery that may never be solved.

The navigational instincts of birds remain a mystery to humans.

Big Cats

MANY REPORTS involving sightings of big cats occur in countries not associated with such animals. In England, where the wild cat is believed to have been extinct for more than 70 years, reports of creatures described as pumas, leopards and panthers are on the increase. Theories proposed to explain reports of big cats include suggestions that they are:

• Escaped zoo or circus animals which have managed to establish a local population, perhaps by cross-breeding with other cats. However, studies show that there is little evidence of such wild-cat populations, particularly in England.

• Survivors of an ancient species, thought to be extinct. This theory has been widely disputed because large cats would require large kills, in the form of deer, sheep or other animals. There seems to be no regular disappearance of such animals.

• Nothing more than misidentification of feral cats, domestic cats, or other animals.

• They may also be big cats living wild: many sightings in the UK are in fact thought to be of former pets released into the wild when the laws on keeping dangerous animals were tightened.

All that is definite is that we still do not know why and how these cats appear, and the number of reputable witnesses claiming to have seen them is increasing.

Tracks of a big cat in the snow in south-west England; the distance between the sets of marks measured 1.3 m (54 in).

An out-of-place kangaroo or wallaby, photographed in 1978 in Wisconsin.

OUT-OF-PLACE ANIMALS

Claims of kangaroos in North Carolina or penguins in New Jersey may sound implausible but, according to Loren Coleman, a psychiatric social worker and cryptozoologist, who has studied hundreds of these cases, there is an answer. He believes these animals may have somehow been teleported from one location to another. 'There's a random pattern to these things,' he says. 'Sometimes these animals literally come out of the blue.' He points out that he has investigated hundreds of sightings, talking to game wardens, police and witnesses. While there is a logical explanation in more than half the cases, at least 20 per cent of the sightings remain enigmas.

Crop circles have become the phenomenon of the late-twentieth century.

Crop Circles

STARTING IN THE middle of the 1980s, rural England experienced a spate of unusual phenomena in fields across the country. Reports came flooding in of perfect circles or complex patterns of flattened crops that were clearly defined. Immediately the UFO brigade suggested that they were evidence of alien spacecraft, which had either landed or hovered. However, there may be many other explanations. At present, the experts are divided on what causes this phenomenon. The main theories include:

- Hoaxes. It was established that parties of hoaxers were entering cornfields to confound the so-called experts. They often succeeded, but many of these hoaxers confessed.
- Hedgehogs, rabbits, the Devil, fairies, ancient Earth power lines, helicopters and whirlwinds have all been blamed.

- It has been suggested that the circles were somehow linked to disturbances in the Earth's magnetic field.
- In August 2000, Colin Andrews, a researcher funded by the Rockerfeller Institute, agreed with this for simple circles but dismissed complex circles as hoaxes.
- Consultant meteorologist Dr Terence Meaden, head of the Tornado and Storm Research Organisation (TORRO) in the UK, believed that unusual air vortices were a factor behind many of the earlier, simpler circles.
- 'Landscape art', created by artists rather than hoaxers.

JUST A JOKE?

IN 1991, an explanation came to light that satisfied many people. Two retired artists, Doug Bower and Dave Chorley, admitted that they had been responsible for the first crop circles. They successfully produced another circle on film, to prove their confession. Naturally other hoaxers had taken up the idea and Doug and Dave believed that there were no genuinely supernatural circles. Between them they had created more than 200 crop circles.
They did admit, however, that they based the pictograms on similar shapes that they had seen in the Australian bush – the origins of which have never been satisfactorily explained.

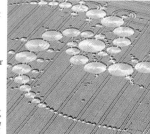

Crop circles at Windmill Hill, Avebury, Wiltshire, southern England, photographed in 1996.

The Siberian Fireball

JUST AFTER 7 a.m. on 30 June 1908, a huge fireball struck the snow-swept tundra of Siberia, incinerating all life over a 65-km (40-mile) area. In seconds, the sparsely inhabited Tunguska River valley was destroyed. Farmer Sergei Semenov was one of the few witnesses whose recollections of the disaster were recorded. He

The mystery explosion over the Siberian forest in 1908.

was some 80 km (50 miles) from the centre of the blast when it happened. He wrote: 'There appeared a great flash. There was so much heat, my shirt was almost burnt off my back. I saw a huge ball of fire that covered an enormous part of the sky. Afterwards it became very dark. It shook the whole house and moved it from its foundations.'

Russian investigators were astonished by the sight. Herds of reindeer were literally roasted where they stood grazing. Trees were felled and nomadic tribesmen over 70 km (45 miles) away from the centre of the blast had been lifted into the air and their tents blown away. It was, beyond doubt, the greatest unexplained disaster ever recorded. In the town of Kirensk, survivors told of a pillar of fire (like the mushroom cloud of a nuclear explosion) rising above the devastation, and people described the River Kan as 'foaming and broiling like a tormented sea'.

UFOs?

MINERALOGIST PROFESSOR Leonid Kulik of the Soviet Academy of Science claimed that a mega-meteorite must have hit the Earth. Since that time, however, this theory has been scorned. There was no massive crater and little evidence of meteorite dust. Theories about the cause of the blast abound. Some people suggest that a spaceship visiting the Earth blew up and that its nuclear reactor exploded. Although the UFO theory has been widely discounted, there is evidence suggesting that the blast could have been nuclear – before man had mastered the splitting of the atom. The Earth's magnetic field was disturbed after the blast, just as it would be after nuclear bomb tests in the future. Furthermore, after a nuclear blast, there are tiny green globules of melted dust, called trinites. These were found after the Russian blast, and experts confirmed that the trinites did not come from the Tunguska River valley. This seems to confirm the experts' opinion that it could have been some form of nuclear explosion.

The devastation left after the unexplained Siberian fireball.

OTHER THEORIES

A NUMBER of other theories have been put forward to explain the occurrence. These include:

- A black hole. Little is known of black hole phenomena, but their gravitational pull is so strong that no light escapes. According to American physicist John Carlson: 'A massive atom-sized black hole entering the Earth's atmosphere at a typical collision velocity for an interplanetary body would create an atmospheric shock wave with enough force to raze hundreds of square kilometres of Siberian forest, ionise air, produce flash-burning and seismic effects. No major crater or meteoritic residue would result.'

- A meteorite. Some scientists say that the blast could have been caused by a giant meteorite that exploded before hitting the ground. The effect would have been like that of a giant shrapnel shell, burning the area around it but creating no crater.

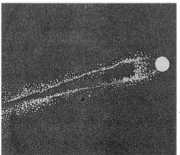

Theories abound to explain the fireball: some believe that it could have been a meteorite (left) or a comet (above right), crashing to Earth.

- A comet. Similar to the meteorite theory is the comet theory detailed in a 1977 paper. In it, two British university professors say that the energy of a comet would have been too low for a full-scale nuclear explosion, but that it could have created a blast of almost the size of an atom bomb. No comets or meteorites were detected in the skies at the time of the explosion, but the academics say that this could be due to the comet only becoming visible to the naked eye at dawn, which would have made it indistinguishable from the sun.

  Despite the plethora of theories, nearly a century of scientific study has failed to come up with a conclusive cause for the Siberian disaster.

Hessdalen Lights

IN NOVEMBER 1981, the inhabitants of the Hessdalen
Valley, stretching across 12 km (7.5 miles) of central Norway,
near the Swedish border, began to experience strange luminous
phenomena. The lights sometimes appeared as frequently as
four times a day, often below the horizon, along mountain tops,
or on the roofs of houses. Usually white or yellowish, they were
typically cigar-shaped, or like spheres or vortices. Occasionally,
a red light maintained a position in front. The lights hovered,
sometimes for up to an hour, and then left at great speed.

PROJECT HESSDALEN

IN 1984, a team of experts calling themselves 'Project
Hessdalen' trekked to the valley and with a great deal of
technological equipment, set out to either establish the presence
of UFOs, or to find another cause for the phenomenon. For
several weeks they investigated the area, recording and measuring
the lights, some of which were red and blue in colour. On 12
February 1985, the lights seemed to respond when laser beams
were flashed at them. One of the objects changed its regular

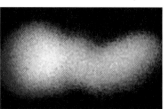

flashing light to
a regular double
flashing light until
the investigators
changed the rhythm
back again.

*One of the mysterious
lights in the Hessdalen
Valley in Norway.*

A researcher at work trying to solve the puzzle of the unexplained Hessdalen lights.

The expedition produced excellent photographs and other readings of the structure of these phenomena. Later research suggested that they were witnessing a type of atmospheric plasma somehow generated in the area, but whose origin was unknown.

In 1986, the lights subsided. A University of Oslo physicist, Elvand Thrane, who had participated in the research, later said, 'I'm sure the lights were real. It's a pity we cannot explain them'.

Other Phenomena

INSTANT HEAT WAVE

ON THE MORNING of 7 July 1987, the temperature in Greensburg, Kansas, rose 11°C (20 °F) in just 10 minutes. At 7.30 a.m. it was 24 °C (75°F), and at 7.40 it was 35 °C (95 °F). John May, National Weather Service meteorologist at Topeka, had never heard of such a phenomenon, but speculated that the layer of cool air that normally develops overnight close to the ground simply switched places with warmer air thousands of metres up. 'We are not sure why this happens,' he said.

BALL LIGHTNING

BALL LIGHTNING is a little-understood phenomenon, usually lasting less than five seconds. It is generally spherical, ranging from 1 to more than 100 cm (0.4 to more than 40 in) in diameter. The balls are reported to move at a few metres per second and to decay silently or with a small explosion. In January 1984, a Russian passenger plane experienced the phenomenon. The crew saw a glowing light several inches in diameter in front of the cockpit. It suddenly disappeared with a loud roar, and reappeared seconds later – after piercing the fuselage in some odd way – in the passengers' cabin. As the passengers watched in disbelief, the spherical object flew above their heads until it reached the tail of the plane, where it divided into two glowing crescents. The crescents then merged into a single sphere and disappeared. Later, when mechanics examined the aircraft, they found a hole in the front of the fuselage and another in the tail.

Some experts claim that ball lightning does not exist, attributing the phenomenon instead to extra-terrestrial activity.

ICE COLD

ON 11 MARCH 1978, at 10.30 a.m., workers in fields at Becquerel, France, heard a loud explosion, followed by the sound of something falling. They rushed to the site and came across a fresh crater containing a 25-kg (11-lb) lump of transparent ice with 'greenish depths'. The lump stayed intact for an hour.

A possible example of ball lightning, photographed at Vorarlberg in Austria in 1978.

COMPENDIUM

The Unexplained on Film

UNEXPLAINED PHENOMENA provide the perfect vehicle for film, which can re-create the fantastic and make it believable. Has the growth of the film industry sparked imaginations and led to our current fascination with the unknown? Are we more able to imagine and therefore see unexplained and unexpected phenomena when we have this point of reference? Many of these films also have other themes including gods or goddesses, ghosts, apparitions, spirits, miracles, and other similar ideas or depictions of extraordinary incidents. They may be combined with other genres, including comedy or horror. Interestingly, however, supernatural films are usually presented in a comical, whimsical or romantic fashion, and are often not designed to frighten the audience.

Brief discussions follow of the most popular films about unexplained phenomena from each decade since the 1950s, each with a list of recommended viewing from that era.

The Creature from the Black Lagoon.

THE 1950s:
THE CREATURE FROM THE BLACK LAGOON

THE QUINTESSENTIAL 1950s' monster movie, *The Creature from the Black Lagoon* (1954) deals with one of the most popular of all unexplained phenomena – monsters from the deep. In this film, the creature (half man, half fish), is a vicious, woman-stealing beast. In reality, many people look rather affectionately on creatures such as the Loch Ness Monster or Ogopogo, but the idea of such life-forms existing in the dark recesses of the ocean is one that has captured the imagination of film-makers for many years.

FILMS OF THE 1950s

20,000 Leagues Under the Sea (1954)
Beast From 20,000 Fathoms, The (1953)
Blob, The (1958)
Curse of Frankenstein, The (1957)
Curse of the Demon (1957)
Day the Earth Stood Still, The (1951)
Destination Moon (1950)
Donovan's Brain (1953)
Forbidden Planet (1956)
House of Wax (1953)
House on Haunted Hill (1958)
Invaders from Mars (1953)
It Came from Beneath the Sea (1955)
It Came from Outer Space (1953)
Journey to the Centre of the Earth (1959)
This Island Earth (1955)
When Worlds Collide (1951)

THE 1960s: *THE BIRDS*

ALFRED HITCHCOCK'S dark and brooding suspense movie *The Birds* (1963) takes nature and gives it human characteristics (and evil ones at that). A flock of birds make unexplained attacks on human beings. They are organised, tactical and inescapable. Like many of Hitchcock's films, *The Birds* is uncomfortable – an unlikely situation that somehow seems possible.

FILMS OF THE 1960s

2001: A Space Odyssey (1968)
Burn Witch, Burn! (1962)
Carnival of Souls (1962)
Damned, The (1963)
Failsafe (1964)
Fantastic Voyage (1966)
First Men in the Moon (1964)
Mysterious Island (1964)
Night of the Living Dead (1968)
Planet of the Apes (1968)
Quatermass and the Pit (1967)
Repulsion (1965)
Seconds (1966)
Village of the Damned (1960)
Voyage to the Bottom of the Sea (1961)

THE 1970s: *CLOSE ENCOUNTERS OF THE THIRD KIND*

STEVEN SPIELBERG'S classic film *Close Encounters of the Third Kind* (1977) was a landmark in the development of science fiction movies. Spielberg worked with a team of UFO experts in order to come up with a story that was realistic. He based many of the incidents in the film on actual case-studies of UFO sightings. The title of the film reflects a UFO classification: encounters of the third kind cover sightings of UFOs and alien beings.

FILMS OF THE 1970s

Alien (1979)
Amityville Horror, The (1979)
Andromeda Strain, The (1971)
Carrie (1976)
Changeling, The (1979)
Colossus – The Forbin Project (1970)
Dark Star (1974)
Dawn of the Dead (1978)
Death Race 2000 (1975)
Deliverance (1972)
Don't Look Now (1973)
Haloween (1978)
It's Alive (1974)
Nosferatu the Vampyre (1979)
Phantasm (1979)
Silent Running (1971)
Sisters (1973)
Soylent Green (1973)
Suspiria (1977)
THX 1138 (1971)
Westworld (1973)

Close Encounters of the Third Kind.

THE 1980s: *ET: THE EXTRA-TERRESTRIAL*

SPIELBERG'S NEXT foray into the world of science-fiction was a fantasy adventure about a young boy who befriends an alien being who has been left behind after his spaceship has returned to his own planet. *ET: the Extra-Terrestrial* (1982) is still a popular classic – a vision of what we hope alien life forms are really like....

FILMS OF THE 1980s

2010: The Year We Make Contact (1984)
Abyss, The (1989)
Aliens (1986)
Altered States (1980)
Back to the Future (1985)
Communion (1989)
Day of the Dead (1985)
Dead Ringers (1988)
Dead Zone, The (1983)
Dressed to Kill (1980)
Dune (1984)
Field of Dreams (1989)
Ghost Story (1981)
Ghostbusters (1984)
Gremlins (1984)
Hangar 18 (1980)
Innerspace (1987)
Legend (1985)
Nightmare on Elm Street, A (1984)
Poltergeist (1982)
Scanners (1981)
Somewhere in Time (1981)
Time Bandits (1981)

ET: The Extra-Terrestrial.

THE 1990s: *THE SIXTH SENSE*

THE INTENSE psychological thriller *The Sixth Sense* (1999), directed by M. Night Shyamalan, is one of a new generation of films about the unexplained. A child psychologist tries to help a young boy who is haunted by ghosts, often of a disturbing nature. The twist in the tale made this film an instant classic.

FILMS OF THE 1990s

Blair Witch Project, The (1999)
Bram Stoker's Dracula (1992)
Contact (1997)
Dark City (1998)
Fairy Tale (1999)
Fire in the Sky (1993)
Flatliners (1990)
Gattaca (1997)
Ghost (1990)
Independence Day (1996)
Interview with the Vampire (1994)
Mars Attacks! (1996)
Men in Black (1997)
Midsummer Night's Dream, A (1999)
Outbreak (1995)
Roswell: The UFO Coverup (1994)
Species (1995)
Starship Troopers (1997)
Timecop (1994)

Further Investigations

THERE IS a wide variety of excellent websites and books devoted to unexplained phenomena. These include:

WEBSITES

Active Mind: The Mysterious and Unexplained:
http://www.activemind.com/Mysterious/

Alien Jump Station: http://area51.upsu.phym.ac.uk/

American Society for Psychical Research: http://www.aspr.com/

Bermuda Triangle: http://icarus.cc.uic.educ/

Centre for UFO Studies: http://www.cufos.org/

Crop Circle Connector: http:///www.nh.ultranet.com/

Faerie Encyclopaedia: http://www.geocities.com/Area 51/Cavern/3351

Global Bigfoot Encyclopaedia:
http://www.planetc.com/users/bigfoot/scott.htm/

Institute for UFO Research: http://isur.com/

Loch Ness Monster Exhibition Centre: http://www.lochness.co.uk/

Paranormal Science Investigations:
http://www.tenthmuse.com/paranormal/index.html

Sea Serpents and Lake Monsters:
http://www.serve.com/shadows/serpent.htm/

Society for Psychical Research: http:/moebius.psy.ed.ac.uk/spr.html/

The Miracles Page: http://www.mcn.org/1/miracles

The Shadowlands: http://theshadowlands.net/mystery.htm

UFO Abductions:
http://ntawwaab.compuserve.com/homepage/AndyPage/
abductio.htm/

The X-Files: http://www.thex-files.com/

The Unexplained Site: http://www.theunexplainedsite.com/

BOOKS

Andrews, Colin and Delgado, Pat, *Circular Evidence*, Bloomsbury, 1989

Baker, Alan, *The Encyclopaedia of Alien Encounters*, Virgin, 1999

Begg, Paul, *Into Thin Air*, David & Charles, 1979

Berlitz, Charles, *The Bermuda Triangle*, Doubleday, 1974

Bord, Janet and Colin, *Alien Animals*, Grafton, 1981

Bord, Janet and Colin, *Modern Mysteries of Britain*, Grafton, 1987

Bord, Janet and Colin, *Modern Mysteries of the World*, Grafton, 1989

Bord, Janet and Colin, *The World of the Unexplained*, Blandford, 1998

Clark, David, *Vanished!*, Michael O'Mara Books, 1994

Clark, Jerome, *The UFO Encyclopaedia*, Omnigraphics, 1994

Devereux, Paul, *Earthlights Revelation*, Blandford, 1989

Doyle, Arthur Conan, *The Coming of the Fairies*, Doran, 1922

Hough, Peter and Randles, Jenny, *Spontaneous Human Combustion*, Robert Hale, 1992

Moore, Bill and Berlitz, Charles, *The Philadelphia Experiment*, Grafton, 1979

Nickell, Joe and Fischer, John, *Secrets of the Supernatural*, Prometheus, 1988

Randles, Jenny, *UFOs and How to See Them*, Anaya, 1992

Randles, Jenny, *Paranormal Source Book*, Piatkus, 1996

Randles, Jenny, *The Complete Book of Aliens and Abductions*, Piatkus, 1999

Spencer, John and Anne, *The Encyclopaedia of the World's Greatest Mysteries*, Headline, 1995

Underwood, Peter, *Peter Underwood's Guide to Ghosts & Haunted Places*, Piatkus, 1999

Watson, Lyall, *Supernature*, Hodder & Stoughton, 1975

Watson, Lyall, *The True Life X-Files*, Eddison Sadd, 1991

Welfare, Simon and Fairley, John, *Arthur C. Clarke's A–Z of Mysteries*, HarperCollins, 1994

Wilson, Ian, *Mind Out of Time*, Gollancz, 1981

Witchell, Nicholas, *The Loch Ness Story*, Penguin, 1991

Index